T0147035

The Jingle Man

LAWRENCE SICURELLA

iUniverse

THE JINGLE MAN

iUniverse books may be ordered through booksellers or by contacting:

iUniverse
1663 Liberty Drive
Bloomington, IN 47403
www.iuniverse.com
1-800-Authors (1-800-288-4677)

Because of the dynamic nature of the Internet, any web addresses or links contained in this book may have changed since publication and may no longer be valid. The views expressed in this work are solely those of the author and do not necessarily reflect the views of the publisher, and the publisher hereby disclaims any responsibility for them.

The views expressed in this work are solely those of the author and do not necessarily reflect the views of the publisher, and the publisher hereby disclaims any responsibility for them.

Any people depicted in stock imagery provided by Getty Images are models, and such images are being used for illustrative purposes only. Certain stock imagery © Getty Images.

ISBN: 978-1-5320-7275-8 (sc)
ISBN: 978-1-5320-7276-5 (e)

Library of Congress Control Number: 2019907694

Print information available on the last page.

iUniverse rev. date: 06/13/2019

CONTENTS

TIME OUT

Take a walk with your dog go smell some flowers
Take a time out from life for a couple of hours
Try to stay focused, ignore the world's wrath
Hear the birds sing as you walk down a path
There's no need for doctors or advice from a shrink
Just throw on some skates and go to a rink
It's never too late we must be diverse
The division and hate we must try to reverse
Turn off your TV get lost in a book
Sit by a stream or fish in a brook
Take a ride in the country smell the fresh air
Visit a farm or an old county fair
Give back to your country it feels really good
Volunteer your time I think everyone should
There's no time for pity stand up and be strong
Enjoy every moment our time here isn't long
As I look at our children our future looks great
Love prevails there's no room for hate
So, fly free like the monarch and cherish each day
Respect one another and we'll all be okay!

FROM PILOT CONTROL

This is pilot control Flight 3407
The weather looks fine as we now enter heaven
We had a safe flight though we did come in late
When we depart from the plane there's St. Peters gate
The Lord just informed us of prayers sent to heaven
They were sent by our loved ones of flight 3407
We took a small detour but there's nothing to fear
The Lord will make sure were all safe up here
We see churches full as you say their goodbyes
We see sadness and tears in everyone's eyes
To each father mother husband and wife
Be happy for us go on with your life
Though we're no longer with you we won't be apart
As long as the memories are still in your heart
That's our gift to you as our lord shows the way
He assures that we'll all be together some day
Our legacy lives on in each one of you
So, encourage your children in whatever they do
Put on your best smile, and don't get depressed
We're with our dear Jesus our sins all confessed
It's amazing up here there's no snow or ice
There's a beautiful garden in paradise
There's so much to tell you but there is this one thing
We'll be with you in worship and whenever you sing
Know that we're always thinking of you,
And know we're beside you in whatever you do
Though it's time to sign off from Flight 3407
Remember us always we'll be smiling from heaven

STARRY STARRY NIGHT

On this glorious night on Flagler Beach
The stars so close you feel you can reach
The ocean waves are the only sound
It's late at night there's no one around
As we lay on the hot orange summer sand
I realize I am one lucky man
A beautiful woman a star filled night
A bright full moon will give us some light
Our problems wash away with each ocean wave
The memories this night forever we'll save
I know there's a God, how else could this be
It's heaven on earth its' serenity
This night can never be taken away
I wish we could stay all night and day
Someday we'll look back and both reflect
It's a special night we'll never forget
Your gorgeous body against the moons shiny light
Your long black hair what a beautiful sight
All the treasures we want are here on the beach
The pleasures we shared were enjoyed by each
A piece of mind the calm in the air
It's a night we both forever we'll share
Just you I and the ocean tide
Laying on the sand side by side
When we're together or if we're apart
It's these special moments stored away in our heart
I'll remember this night wherever you are
And I'll think of you always with each shooting star.

MY PICKUP TRUCK

It was Saturday night at our favorite bar
I took my girl out she looked like a star
I put a quarter in the jukebox I played our song
As I looked around something was wrong
This guy was slow dancing with my girl
It made me so crazy my head in a swirl
So I ordered the strongest drink in the house
Then I went on over to talk to this louse
But to my surprise my girlfriend stepped in
She talked real bold as she drank her gin
I'll never forget it came out of the blue
She said "He's not to blame" then she said we were through
She broke my heart I could feel the pain
She flushed fifteen years right down the drain
She loved me no more, that was a fact
She left with this guy she never looked back
I drank all night till the early morn
When I awoke my head was on my car horn
My head was pounding my girl was gone
My life turned into a country song
I got in my car with my coffee cup
As I drove down the road, I saw this cool truck
It looked really sharp and it was for sale
So I bought the truck to forget my gal
I quit my job and headed west
I would start a new life and forget the rest
When I went through Vegas with my new pickup truck
I went to a casino to try my luck
As luck would have it, I began to win
I won enough money to start over again
I drove my truck all the way to the coast
Now I'm no bragger but I must boast
I'm no longer in Buffalo in the freezing snow
I found a great woman have lots of dough
I now have a great job I make a good buck
And I owe it all to my new pickup truck!

YESTERDAY

Andy Griffith, Gomer Pile, and the Lucy show
We watched mom make pizza, as she rolled out the dough
Skipping stones with our dog, in our backyard pond
By eight p.m. we had our PJ's on
If we're good mom would make us her apple pie
Life was real simple in sixty nine
Years flew by, mom and dad passed away
But the values they taught are with us today
I loved sixties music, I must confess
"Let it be" by the Beatles is the song I loved best
A ride in the country, on Sunday at noon
I remember Neil Armstrong's walk on the moon
Fifteen cent burgers are a thing of the past
We must slow down, we move way to fast
We have E-mail and texting, we no longer write letters
I'd love to go back, where things were much better
They tore down the Drive In, to put up a mall
They're open on Sundays, that says it all
If I could turn back the clock, life's lessons I'd borrow
I'd find a cure for diseases, and rid us of sorrow
So many things have changed, where do I start
It's the memories I saved, that I stored in my heart

RED, RED WINE

Red, red wine is what I desire
It mellows me out, I am a live wire
I love a Shiraz or a glass of merlot
Sometimes I drink a bottle or so
After a run when my bones are all achy
Or I have a bad day and feel I bit shaky
Red red wine is quite an escape
Who'd think all this fun could come from a grape
Why I love my red wine still isn't clear
But my glass of merlot sure beats a warm beer
I've spilled a few glasses over the years
A spilled glass of Merlot brought this lady to tears
I wish this poor lady at least cracked a smile
When I spilled my red wine, I did it with style
I cleaned her beige couch, but she was really mad
I won't see her again which makes me real glad
This cranky old lady should try a merlot
Then relax, have fun, and let herself go!

THE JINGLE MAN

Wherever I go, wherever I roam
I write cute jingles, and recite my poems
I make people happy, I make children smile
I make them forget life for a while
If you give me your ear for a second or two
I could put you in a really good mood
I can help you escape reality sometimes
You'll laugh out loud when you read my rhymes
I'd like to take you around the world
Or beneath the sea searching for pearls
I make people laugh, and I make people cry
I can change how you feel if I try
I can write fiction, or I can write fact
And I'll keep you all guessing 'til the very last act
I can give you chills, or break your heart
It depends on my mood when I start
I'll take you places you've never been
If you like these places you can go there again
My poems can be lengthy, but that's no surprise
And you may need a hanky to wipe tears from your eyes
I'm the jingle man, that's what I do
I get lost in my poems for an hour or two
I only can write what's in my heart
I must have an idea before I can start
Writing these poems is what I love
But my talent comes from heaven above.

RAINBOW OF LOVE

It was the most colorful rainbow I ever saw
It was just hanging over Niagara Falls
It looked like it came from heaven above
The feeling it brought was a feeling of love
At the end of that rainbow is where we should be
It's where people go to feel totally free
It's where Grandma and Grandpa are very young
It's where birds are chirping and songs are sung
It's a place with no cancer, illness or pain
It's where there is sunshine, never any rain
It's a peaceful place, there are no wars
There are no houses, with windows and doors
There is just happiness, it's very serene
There is a rose garden, it's a beautiful scene
There's no room for sorrow, or any self pity
It's the closest thing to Emerald City
You can walk in through, the big white gate
You're always welcome, you're never too late
Just come on in, you can take off your shoes
Everyone's welcome, there aren't any rules
Its peace and tranquility forever and ever
You'll be with your loved ones, you'll all be together
So next time you see that rainbow in the sky
Remember that's where the bluebirds fly.

THE OLD OAK TREE

I'll never forget the day I turned eight
It was time for my presents, I could hardly wait
It was the best birthday I ever had
The very last present would be from my dad
As my dad took my hand, he said this to me
"My present to you is this little Oak tree"
Someday I promise you will understand
Your tree will still be here when you are a man
So dad got a shovel, and we dug a deep hole
It took us about an hour or so
When the oak tree was planted, dad looked to the sky
He said "Happy birthday" with a tear in his eye
Like your tree you will grow and become a young man
And remember I'll always be your biggest fan
I planted this tree with all of my love
It will grow with the grace of our dear lord above
When dad looked at me I could tell he was proud
As we both hugged, there wasn't a sound
It's a moment I'll cherish the rest of my life
I'll share this someday with my children and wife
The years flew by and the tree grew tall
We promised we'd meet here each year in the fall
Our bond was as strong as the roots of the tree
Dad was my hero and always will be
Like my tree I thought dad would live forever
I never knew anyone as witty and clever
I'll never forget when I got the call
The leaves were falling, it was early fall
It was my dear mom, and she sounded so sad
From the sound of her voice, I knew it was dad
The doctors all said "We don't have an answer"
They said that my dad had a rare type of cancer
As I sat by his side, his last words he would say
"When you sit by your tree you will be okay"
Dad said he loved me with a tear in his eye
"When you come there each fall, look up to the sky
You will then know I'm sitting by our Lord's side
And peace and serenity is what you will find.

CONGO, WAVES AND SAND

The crystal white sand, the waves and my drum
The bright full moon and a bottle of rum
As the tide hit's the shore, the moon shines its light
With the heavenly stars, it's a beautiful sight
I take off my sandals, run my toes through the sand
I dream I play drums for a great Latin band
The beat of my drum floats through the air
There is a real calmness, I don't have a care
The peace and tranquility is hard to explain
I feel ten years younger, I have no more pain
My mind has been cleansed, my vision is clear
My problems seem small as the waves hit the pier
My drum beat gets louder, it has a nice tone
I'm here by myself, yet I don't feel alone
I have god given talent, it was heaven sent
It just took a while to know what this all meant
I now know there's more than just money and fame
A lot of things changed, yet a lot stayed the same
So give me my drum, the moon and the beach
The stars so close, I feel I could reach
There's no better place I'd rather be
For my piece of mind and serenity.

LONLEY PICKLE

As a lonely pickle, stuck in this pickle jar
I wish I could go party, at the local salad bar
My friends say I'm a bragger, my stories I embellish
They say if I don't change my ways, someday I will be relish
If you put me on a burger, it's a taste that can't be beat
I know I am no "Dill", but my girlfriend thinks I'm "Sweet"

"MOM" ARCH BUTTERFLY

The angels took mom two years ago
A day didn't go by that I missed her so
Was she cancer free did her pain finally cease
Was she at the Lord's side, was mom now at peace
Then one beautiful warm summer day
A monarch butterfly glided my way
While jogging in the park mile after mile
This monarch stayed with me for quite a while
I can't explain it, but it was meant to be
This beautiful butterfly looked peaceful and free
I knew it was mom, as I wiped a tear
Mom was alright, this became clear
At that moment I felt though we were apart
She never really left, she was there in my heart
As I continued to run, and the monarch just flew
I felt mom was there to help me get through
How graceful this monarch seemed to glide
As she stayed with me, right by my side
I felt mom's presence, I was alone no longer
I felt I could cope, I felt much stronger
As the monarch flew so peaceful and free
I felt my mom was hugging me
As the monarch finally flew away
I could almost hear my mother say
"It's been two years, it's time you move on
When you see the monarch, it's me your mom
Like the monarch, you must embrace each day
And don't be afraid to do it your way
We're all God's children, he made us unique
Follow the monarch, if it's peace that you seek
Fill each day with laughter and love
I'm your "MOM" Arch butterfly from heaven above
I knew from that day my heart would now mend
And someday in heaven I'd see mom again
So when I see a monarch, and its colorful wings
I think of the love and beauty it brings.

DAD'S LAST LETTER

My Dad went away when I was just three
He fought for our country so we could be free
Dad was a hero, he was very brave
Mom read all dads letters, each one that she saved
I'm now twenty one how the years seem to fly
Sometimes late at night, I still hear mom cry
Mom never remarried though it's been many years
She still has the heartache I still see her tears
I hope that someday I'm just like my dad
I pray that I have the courage he had
I don't want my mom to worry about me
Cause I know someday a soldier I'll be
Mom understood the day that I told her
She hugged me & cried then said be a good soldier
I promised my mom that I'd make her proud
She then gave me a letter that she had found
If you're reading this son I'm probably not here
I didn't die in vain and never showed fear
Take care of your mom you must remain strong
I'm standing beside you even though I am gone
I tried to stay safe I died with my gun
When you fight for our country, be safe my son
Someday up in heaven we'll meet once again
Until that day do the best that you can
I love you my son I'll watch over you
Tell your children that grandpa bled red white and blue

ALABAMA

I'm heading down south to Alabama
And all I have packed is a pear and banana
With no gas in the tank, and the clothes on my back
I have just enough money to buy a twelve pack
I have to get away from this frigid cold
These long nasty winters are taking a toll
I'm driving down south to trust my luck
The only thing I own is my pickup truck
As I'm cruising the highway I have this one thought
I better slow down, before I get caught
I start to daydream about my new life
Thank God I'm single and don't have a wife
When I finally arrive at my destination
I think I'll kick back and take a vacation
I've been working each day for 35 years
In that cold dreary factory I left a few tears
I'm a blue collar guy with white collar mind
An exciting vocation I soon will find
At the factory I had to punch a time card
I was never late and I always worked hard
Then one day they closed their doors
We found out that day we weren't working no more
I thinks it's an omen it's time for a change
It's time to move on & rearrange
As my truck got closer to the Alabama state line
I smelled some southern food being fried
So I stopped at this diner for southern fried chicken
It sure was delicious, it was finger licking
With that southern fried taste still in my mouth
I felt I belonged in the beautiful south
Now all that I need is a job and a dog
And a nice little fireplace to throw on a log

JUST ANOTHER COUNTRY SONG

The jukebox is playing a sad country song
The words make you cry how things can go so wrong
Aren't any country singers ever happy?
Some of their songs get pretty sappy
Who's cheating who, who stole your wife
Does every country singer have a sad life?
If it's someone's misfortune you want to hear
Put on a county song you'll have tears in your beer
Your life will look better than the one in the song
But you'll get depressed it won't take long
There's lying and cheating and lots of remorse
There's a cowboy and his woman a dog and a horse
Your friend can't be trusted he took off with your girl
They went to México and your heads in a swirl
To make matters worse they took all your money
It's only a song but this isn't funny
I love Carrie Underwood her songs are the best
But some of her songs leave me depressed
Can we hear some happiness for a change?
Could we hear that old classic home on the range?
Could we hear some songs that don't make us sore?
Or a song that don't make me want to drink more
Could you please not sing about your old dog dying?
Or your wife doesn't love you, you know she is lying
Could you please not sing about the sick little girl?
Or your dying friend who's name is Earl
Could we hear a song where things go right?
Your wife still loves you and she looks out of sight
Could you sing about our country but not make me cry
Could you sing me to sleep with a sweet lullaby?
I'm a big country fan and I'll always be
I thank God I'm an American where at least I am free

AN OLD COUNRY SONG

Everywhere I go I hear bad news
All my friends are singing the blues
I had a good life until things went wrong
My life is like an old country song
My woman is leaving she's packed her bags
I'm older and balder and my stomach sags
My kids move away and my dog loves my wife
I never figured on this kind of life
My neighbors are lazy they don't cut their grass
My patience is really running out fast
My job really stinks my boss is a jerk
Getting drunk Friday nights is my only perk
I ask myself what happened to me
I married too young but that's history
I pay alimony and child support
Once a month I go to court
I count my blessings I still have my health
Even though my ex-wife has all my wealth
I often complain but nobody hears
I'm better off having a couple of beers
In county songs lives turn around
For now I'll stay in this little town
Folks know my business, but I don't care
Let them all talk and let them stare
Someday I might just leave in my truck
I'll head out west and try my luck
I have a great family and friends I have plenty
If it wasn't for bad luck I wouldn't have any
My last chapters not written this life made me strong
So for now I'll just listen to an old country song

SET 'EM UP JOE

My wife just left me, and I'm all alone
And she took just about everything that I own
I had this feeling right from the start
This woman would someday break my heart
So set 'em up Joe, I'm buying the drinks
My woman is gone, my life really stinks
Put a quarter in the jukebox, play me a song
And I'll try to figure out what I have done wrong
I thought we got married for better or worst
The honeymoon's over, the bubble has burst
She says she still loves me, but she wants a new life
She's tired of being the "faithful wife"
She tells me there isn't another man
But her wedding ring is off her hand
She cries herself to sleep each night
The love is gone, it doesn't feel right
She parties all night, and stays out 'till the morning
She says married life has just gotten boring
So set 'em up Joe with another round
Tonight's the night I do the town
Joe you've always been a good friend
You were with me to the bitter end
This bar has been like a home for me
Everyone treats me like family
As my eyes well up and I wipe away my last tear
I say goodnight and chug my beer
I feel much better, I have peace at last
So if you see my wife tell her "KISS MY ASS"

CAROLINA ON MY MIND

I've traveled through this beautiful land
But I keep coming back to the Carolina sand
The soft white sand is quite appealing
The ocean at night is a powerful feeling
The stars can be seen on a clear summer night
Just like a painting, a glorious sight
Carolina's my home, and always will be
It cleanses my soul, and lets me feel free
I like California and Florida too
But Carolina's in my heart, through and through
The sunset is legend, the people are tan
The weather is perfect, and so is the sand
It's the closest to heaven that I could be
With all its beauty and majesty
I see fishermen fishing out on the pier
Seafood is very plentiful here
So give me a pole and an old pickup truck
I'll go to Carolina and try my luck
As I lay by the ocean and the warm white sand
Life couldn't be better, as I work on my tan!

YASGUR'S FARM

Way back when in sixty nine
There was a concert called Woodstock, it was one of a kind
Max Yasgur lived in Bethel Woods
Where farmers worked hard to peddle their goods
As hippies ascended on Yasgur's farm
A half million came, and the town was alarmed
They came for peace and Rock and Roll
'Nam was ending, or so we were told
Woodstock just happened there was no explanation
Protests have spread across our great nation
There were flower children, bell bottoms were in
The fight against establishment was about to begin
Yasgur gave Woodstock his farm and his land
They spread love, smoked pot, there were rock and roll bands
Shunned by his neighbors, Max took a chance
He gave them a platform to love, sing and dance
On Yasgur's farm great memories were made
It was three days of peace, when the rock bands played
It was Janice, Jimmie, and yes Joe Cocker
And thanks to Max Yasgur, you're now legends and rockers!

OLD STONEY CREEK

I'll never forget, I was six years old
Dad bought me my first fishing pole
Dad loved to go fishing, he'd fish once a week
He'd always go down to Old Stoney Creek
One day he said son, I'll teach you to fish
This was always my number one wish
With my tackle box and my brand new pole
We'd pack the truck, and away we'd go
Fishing with dad, I had lots of fun
We'd sit and talk, I learned a ton
When I caught my first fish I'll never forget
Dad gave me a dollar, because I won the bet
We'd bet on who'd get the first fish of the day
And if dad won he would make me pay
The days we spent fishing we formed a strong bond,
At Stoney Creek, on our favorite pond
It was here dad taught me the values of life
You see Dad was as sharp as a fishing knife
When I got older, we fished a lot less
Those days fishing with Dad were always my best
I now go fishing with my six year old son
We talk about life, we have lots of fun
Dad has been sick, he became really weak
But he still wanted to fish at Old Stoney Creek
When Dad passed away, there we're lots of tears
I can still hear what Dad said over the years
"I'll always be there if its answers you seek
I'll be sitting beside you, at Old Stoney Creek!

BE HUMBLE

(Locker room pep talk)
As athletes we are ready to battle again
Let's move forward, but not forget where we've been
Pray we stay healthy during our quest
Leave it all on the field, let's give it our best
Whenever you feel that you are the star
Stay so humble, don't forget who you are
Let's leave our ego in this room
We are resilient, no gloom and doom
Stay focused, hit hard, and always play smart
The thing they can't measure, is the size of our heart
Let us now bow our heads, hold hands and unite
Play tough, play fair, and keep victory in sight

TRUE LOVE

I thought I found true love, but I was mistaken
Now I'm alone and my heart is aching
You tell me you loved me, but how could that be
You hurt me and took my dignity
I thought you had come from heaven above
You were my angel, as pure as a dove
But like most good things, it came to an end
The day I caught you with my best friend
You said it just happened, it wasn't planned
Now I'm trying to forget you, if only I can
Life must go on, but that's easier said
There are days I couldn't even get out of bed
Then one day I went to this store
I met this girl, and I don't hurt anymore
Now I get what the good Lord was saying
I'd find my true love if I kept praying
So never give up when life looks bleak
Pray to the Lord, if it's true love you seek

OLD BLACKIE

I may not be rich, or have much luck
But one thing I have is my pickup truck
It's black on the outside, with red velvet interior
When I drive my truck, I feel superior
I've had many girlfriends, and one ex-wife
But I had just one truck my whole entire life
She can get me to sixty in a second or so
But I try not to speed, I don't have that much dough
If my truck could talk, your ears would ring
What happens in "Old Blackie", a country star could sing
My truck was faithful, unlike my ex- wife
My truck gave me pleasure, my wife gave my strife
When I drove through town people would stare
Her engine sounded like a roaring bear
No matter how bad my day would be
My truck could get me through misery
I just hop in my truck and hit the gas
Get a case of beer, and forget my past
I head out to my house on the lake
After a few beers, I'm barely awake
There is no woman to yell at me
There's wilderness as far as the eyes can see
"Old Blackie" will always be my best friend
And she'll be with me 'till the very end

IN YOUR HEART, OUT OF THE BOTTLE

It used to be fun, we'd party all night
We were thirty years old, it all seemed all right
But over the years, the fun went away
There would come a time, a price we would pay
Let me back in your heart, and out of this bottle
I promise my dear, it's my last swallow
The luster is gone, and so are you
It's me and this bottle, and I'm feeling blue
We'd party all night, and sometimes the next day
They would make the last call, but we would still stay
We were quite the couple, we were so much in love
You were my sweet angel, from heaven above
But the devil in the bottle, he's been there for years
There were plenty of good times, and just as many tears
We had that in common, we loved to have fun
Mixed with some whiskey and a bottle of rum
It's taken a tow, and at age thirty four
I don't want this kind of life anymore
We still like to drink, but it isn't the same
It feels like we're playing a losing game
I'll make this promise if you would come back
I'll drink no more, and that is a fact
Booze is the devil in disguise
It isn't the truth, it's a bundle of lies
"So let me back in your heart, and out of this bottle
And I promise you dear, this is my last swallow"

MY PONY

When I was young I had a pony
I fed him cheese and macaroni
Every day when I got home from school
I'd ride my pony, he was so cool
I loved my pony, he was my best friend
I try to ride him as much as I can
I missed him when I was in school
And I have to believe he missed me too
While other kids went out to play
It was with my pony I would stay
He had blue eyes like his mother
He was very unique, he was like no other
His big blue eyes were so very cool
That's why I named my pony "Blue"
When I talked to Blue, he understood
He knew me like no other could
One day my parents said to me
It's with your friends you should be
I liked my friends, but I loved my pony
He never got mad, he wasn't a phony
Years went by and Blue got old
He was getting frail, if the truth be told
I couldn't ride him, like I use to do
I missed our rides and so did Blue
Instead of riding we'd take a walk
He listened to me when I would talk
Then one day after school
I went to the stable, but there was no Blue
When I asked my mother, she started to cry
Blue is in "Pony" heaven, up in the sky
I lost my best friend, and though we're apart
Blue will always be here in my heart

MY FROZEN POND

My feet were frozen, so was my nose
I couldn't even feel my toes
We were playing hockey on my backyard pond
It was there my friends and I would bond
We played all day 'til the sun went down
Shooting the puck was the only sound
I remember those days, I was almost ten
Life seemed to be more innocent then
Playing hockey was my childhood dream
I wanted to play for a professional team
Years went by and I grew up
I imagined winning the Stanley Cup
Dad and mom encouraged my dream
Every game I played they were there it would seem
When dad would see me at the rink
He'd smile and give me this little wink
It was then I knew what I had to do
It wasn't just my dream, it was my parents dream too
I went to college, got my education
But I knew some day hockey would be my vocation
When I finished college I told my dad
If I couldn't pay hockey, I wouldn't be sad
That fateful day had finally came
My life would never be the same
I was drafted by the Mighty Ducks
I loved my job, shooting pucks
And through it all over the years
My parents were there to ease all my fears
My friends aren't here, but we still have a bond
And I'll never forget my frozen pond

A MIRACLE IN BAKERSVILLE

(This is a story of a miracle)
It takes place in a town called Bakersville
Liz and Joe Brown were married last year
They bought a small house down by the pier
In this small town there was plenty of joy
When the Browns were blessed with a baby boy
Jacob was born on Christmas day
And for this they thank Jesus whenever they pray
Bakersville was special, there weren't many fears
There was plenty of laughter, not many tears
Then came that fateful day in November
The Browns try to forget, but they'll always remember
Jacob went to the doctor that gloomy day
The Browns couldn't bear what the doctor would say
Little Jacob was dying, he was five years old
He didn't have long to live they were told
Jacob had cancer, and there was no cure
How could this happen to a child so pure
The Browns don't remember, much more that day
They vowed to stay strong, and continue to pray
When the town found out, they did what they could
By now poor Jacob wasn't feeling that good
This horrible disease was taking a toll
The doctors said Jacob had three months or so
The Browns were crushed but they tried to stay strong
They believed in God's arms was where he belonged
I'll never forget, it was Christmas day
The folks of Bakersville came by and prayed
Something real special happened that night
On Jacobs next checkup there was no cancer in sight
Bakersvillle had prayed to our Lord above
The best cure they thought would be the Lords love
The moral of this story is follow the Lord's way
Miracles can happen if you continue to pray
Dedicated to all those stricken by this dreadful disease

CAMELOT

It was the sixties, I'll never forgot
Our lives, they felt like Camelot
There were four young lads from Liverpool
And we pledged to our flag each day in school
Hippies and Flower children were everywhere you went
And John F. Kennedy was our president
We saw Neil Armstrong walk on the moon
And the Woodstock album had some really great tunes
We had prayer in our schools, and family traditions
Our country was never in better condition
Gas was cheap, we drove nice cars
At eighteen years old, we could drink at bar
A shot and a beer, cost a buck fifty
We had some neat words like groovy and nifty
We watched Howdy Doody and Superman
Leave it to Beaver and Peter Pan
The clothes we wore were denim and cotton
Love and peace would not be forgotten
I'd love to go back to Camelot
But stories and memories are all that we got

COWBOY BOOTS AND TIGHT BLUE JEANS

I just worked a double and I'm about to leave
It's Friday night, and I need a reprieve
So I jump in the shower, and attempt to get clean
I put on my boots and tight blue jeans
I'm far from the best looking man around
But this broken down cowboy will tonight paint the town
We all look better at closing time
I'm a single guy, so what's the crime
I'll do some line dancing in my cowboy boots
It takes me back to my Nashville roots
The girls all love me, it could be the jeans
I haven't danced this much since my early teens
At age forty two, I am no spring chicken
But a good country song will get these boots kickin'
A couple of tequilas and a couple of beers
We'll make me feel brave, and ease all my fears
The girls must be drunk, because they think that I'm cute
I'm just an old country boy, with not a lot of loot
I'm not all that smart, but I do trust my luck
As I take this girl home in my new pickup truck
I haven't found that "Right girl" so I keep on looking'
They don't have to be cute, just enjoy some home cooking'
I live a simple life, I don't have a lot
But I thank the dear Jesus for all that I got
I may be single the rest of my life
If I find the right girl, I'd make her my wife
I pray she had beauty inside and out
A nice country girl is what I'm taking about
She'd be full of fun, but not cause a scene
And I know she'd look good in her "Tight blue jeans"

AN OLD MANS KNOWLEDGE

I may have some wrinkles, and my hair may be gray
But like an old book, I have plenty to say
My muscles are weak, and I walk a bit slow
The wear and tear has taken a toll
I now need glasses to see the fine print
I lose things daily, and I don't have a hint
I take a few naps in mid afternoon
I just burnt my dinner, I think it is ruined
My attention span is not there anymore
And things I once did, I can't do like before
But here's one thing, I'm not here to complain
My life has been sunshine and very little pain
I appreciate laughter and my family's love
I can now give my grandchild my old worn out glove
I look for the good, my glass is half full
I may be sixty, but I still am a bull
I jog a lot slower, but I run every day
I follow the path because only I know the way
I still ride my bike two hours a week
Serenity and tranquility is all that I seek
I look a lot older, but I don't much care
I'm sixty years old and I still have my hair
My children, God bless them they make me real proud
The things they accomplished are the treasures I've found
My life has been full, I have no regrets
My family's my wealth, it's as good as it gets
Don't judge an old person, they can teach you so much
They may not look strong but they still pack a punch
Someday when you're old you'll know what I mean
I may have turned sixty but I feel like sixteen
The years go much faster, but I live for today
I may be older, but I have lots to say
So when you see me some day, please stop to talk
Take my hand, let's go for a walk
The things I could tell you, you could write a book
And I won't charge a dime for the knowledge you took

STRAWBERRY SHORTCAKE

It's been twenty three years, I remember the day
The first time I held you I was kind of afraid
You looked like an angel, so pretty and frail
I knew growing up you'd be dad's little gal
You were my sweet little daughter, I helped to create
You were my little strawberry shortcake
Your red rosy cheeks, your red curly hair
Your smile so infectious, so precious and rare
From the scrapes on your knees, while riding your bike
To your very first boyfriend, that you said that you liked
My strawberry shortcake, we shared some tears
From band aids to heartaches, I helped ease your fears
You are now twenty three, there's a man in your life
He wants my shortcake to be his new wife
I told him I knew just how he felt
Strawberry shortcake can make your heart melt
I told him to love her, for better or worse
You see, I am her dad, I saw her first
If you love one another, a great life you'll both make
But remember she'll always be my strawberry shortcake

DUTCH APPLE PIE

I am a Dutch apple pie
I taste so good, I'll make you cry
I'm at my best hot out of the oven
I'm what you call some old fashion lovin'
My apples are fresh, my crust's golden brown
I'm in Ma and Pa's stores, in every small town
You may prefer donuts and that's okay
But there's nothing like pie on a cold wintry day
I've got cinnamon spread all over my crust
Eat me with ice cream if you must
If you see me someday, at your corner store
Buy me and you'll won't be hungry no more
Last but not least, enjoy every bite
Have a big glass of milk, and have a good night

FLAGLER BEACH

The ocean so blue, the stars you can reach
The sand so orange, on Flagler Beach
It's a place for surfing, a place for fishing
A place to relax, a place for wishing
You can eat at the Pier, they serve the best food
There's music at Finns, if you're in the mood
Daytona is only minutes away
It's the most famous beach, or so they say
St' Augustine's near, it's a quaint little town
It's where the oldest buildings and Churches are found
You can smell the ocean, put your toes in the sand
You can lay on the beach, and work on your tan
You can jog by the ocean, or fish off the shore
There's sailing and boat rides, and so much more
So when you're at Flagler beach, wear your best smile
Kick up your feet and do stay a while

A PENNY FOR YOUR THOUGHTS

There are days I wish I could read your mind
As long as your thoughts are sweet and kind
There are days in your mind I dare not wander
But if it's a chance to know you, it's a chance I can't squander
Did you forget to take the dog out last night?
Don't read your wife's mind, it is an unpleasant sight
Did you ever wonder what your dog was thinking'?
He's pretty smart for a dog, but he ain't no Lincoln
What about the apes that live in the zoo
They just hang around, they think they're so cool
Do babies like all that baby talk?
Or being pushed in a stroller, for another long walk
What were you thinking when you came out of the womb
What's King Tut thinking as he lays in his tomb?
I can't read your eyes when they are blinking
And are you just fibbing when you are winking
I really don't know what's on the Lord's mind
But I know he love's us and is very kind

SEPTEMBER MORN

It was an overcast day, the 11th of September
It's a day I know now, I'll always remember
As I glanced outside, things seemed alright
The flowers outside were a beautiful sight
I finished my coffee, headed out the door
Not knowing the day what we had in store
When I got to work, it was a beautiful morning
It was a slow day, a little bit boring
About 10 am we got the news
A plane hit the Trade Center, but there wasn't any clues
When the second plane hit, it was plain to see
We were being attacked, but how could this be
As we listened to the radio, it became clear
Terrorists attacked us, we can all feel the fear
We later found out, the Pentagon was hit
There was this sick feeling in the bottom of my pit
Who were these people, what else would they do
We're going to war, would we all die too
No one had answers, but one thing we knew
We wouldn't back down, we're the red white and blue
Our country is brave, we're as resilient as hell
When the fight begins we'll answer the bell
Well it's seven years later and that day's not forgotten
You can run, but not hide, we'll get you Bin Laden
As a country we're closer, but we still feel the pain
That day lives forever, they didn't die in vain

GRANDPA

(WORDS OF WISDOM)

I learned more from Grandpa, than I did any book
And from his sharp mind, the wisdom I took
He told me stories about prohibition
He worked construction, he had lots of ambition
He was forced to quit school in the fourth grade
He helped his family, with the money he made
He had working man hands, he was a blue collar guy
He was as tough as they come, he never would cry
I went to his house every Saturday morning
We talked for hours, it never got boring
I'd cut grandpa's grass, then have a few beers
We'd laughed so much, it would bring us to tears
Grandpa was humble, though he was very smart
And he loved his grandchildren, with all his heart
He finished his food that we wouldn't eat
And grandma's food couldn't be beat
I miss grandpa's stories, and all that he knew
There's a little of grandpa, in whatever we do
He was a strapping man at six foot three
Yet he was as kind and gentle as you can be
I hope I'm like grandpa when I grow old
And I'll tell my children the stories he told
Even though grandpa did depart
He'll always be with me right here in my heart
It's been ten years since grandpa went away
And I hope to see grandpa in heaven some day

UNFORGETTABLE MEMORIES

Do you remember that first kiss at age sixteen?
Or your first grade teacher you thought was so mean
That smile that girl gave you in study hall
Those were some good times, if I recall
You're very first breakup, you felt real rotten
These are your memories never forgotten
You'll never forget your very first love
It felt so special, it fit like a glove
Or that cheerleader you dated back in tenth grade
Those are all memories that will not fade
You'll never forget your very first car
Or the very first time you drank at a bar
It seemed like yesterday, you started to shave
Do you remember detention, when you didn't behave?
These memories will always be with you
They're fresh in your mind, they feel brand new
You remember playing drums, in your high school band
Your mom and dad were your biggest fans
Now that you're older, you appreciate those times
Sometimes you wonder how you survived
The Viet Nam war, how we were all torn
Miniskirts and bellbottoms were now being worn
Sunday nights, we watched the Ed Sullivan show
Girls were fainting in the very first row
The Beatles were singing, "I want to hold your hand"
There was Beatle mania across our great land
These memories you have, when you're old and gray
They'll be in your heart, and there they will stay

ROAD TRIP

It's Friday afternoon, my boss calls me in
He says my works lacking, and won't tell me again
So on the way home I stop at a bar
I have a few beers, I don't live to far
After hours of drinking, I spent most of my check
I finally went home, my girl was a wreck
She looked really sad, then she stared crying
I told her I'm sorry, but she said I was lying
My dog even gave me an attitude
Nobody here was in a good mood
So I packed my suitcase, kept a stiff upper lip
Called my good friend, and planned a road trip
He was stunned and shocked as he could be
He thought I had the perfect family
He lived alone, so he was ready
I needed a friend who was calm and steady
Then I called my boss and told him I quit
As I hung up the phone, he was having a fit
I told my girl I was going away
I told her I knew that she'd be okay
She clenched her fist, hit me in the lip
It was then I realized this was a permanent trip
So I packed real fast, headed out to the coast
We did pretty good, not meaning to boast
I met this sweet girl, who understood me
I got a job, at this great company
My friend got hitched to this wonderful girl
She looked really cute with her log brown curls
Now every night I sleep like a log
And another good thing, I still have my dog

MISTY

I'll never forget the day you were born
It was misty outside, that September morn
As soon as I saw your big blue eyes
You were Daddy's girl, but that's no surprise
We named you misty, it seemed so right
You were a sweet girl, so precious and bright
You loved country music, since you were just one
You knew how to dance, before you could run
I remember you Misty, at the age of three
How you sang and danced for the family
Then came that fateful day you turned four
You became really sick, you couldn't dance anymore
When they said you were sick, I wiped away some tears
When you asked if you'd be dancing in heaven next year
When the angels came for you, it was early May
I'll never forget, it was a hot misty day
I think of you always, it's so hard to sleep
I have your dance shoes, and forever I'll keep
Then one night in a dream you came to me
You said, "Daddy don't cry, I am now cancer free
I dance in Gods garden, where bluebirds sing songs
I dance with the angels, it's where I belong"
Misty, in my heart, I can feel all your love
I can now see you dancing, in heaven above

DEAR DAUGHTER......FROM MOM

I've taught you everything that I know
Being independent should be your main goal
Someday you'll leave this humbled nest
I hope you'll be ready, I did my best
Don't forget your roots, we'll always be here
And if you follow our Lord, you'll have nothing to fear

MY GRANDPA

I'm not the sharpest tool in the shed
But I learned from my grandpa, and kept my family well fed
After I cut my grandpa's grass
We'd have a few shots, as the day would pass
Grandpa would talk about the old times
He'd tell me about his bootlegging crimes
When grandpa came home from some neighborhood bars
Grandma would let him sleep under the stars
His education was brief, his wisdom was great
He supported his family, made sure they all ate
He was a mountain of a man, and it seemed to me
He was the best role model, there ever could be
His heart was so soft, his hands were like stone
And he was always there if you needed a loan
No one was stronger, or had a stronger will
That made it so hard, when grandpa took ill
Grandma had passed, and he loved her so
But I wasn't ready to let grandpa go
Before Grandpa passed we some great years
We played lots of cards, we shared some tears
I'll never forget when he bought me this watch
And each New Year's Eve we would drink some scotch
I'll take grandpa's wisdom wherever I go
I can't wait to see him, because I miss him so

THE LAZY ELF

Santa was ready to start making toys
Christmas was coming for little girls and boys
The assembly line was all set to go
The season was here, it started to snow
Santa had a meeting, with every last elf
Every elf was energetic except lazy little Ralph
Ralph liked to play, but hated to work
All his fellow elf's thought Ralph was a jerk
With all the elf's working, from morning to night
All the colorful toys, what a wonderful sight
As they worked so hard, every muscle did ache
Santa thought it was time, for a well-deserved break
The elf's were tired, their work almost complete
Santa would have just one more feat
The last toy was hard, where would he start
Though he was lazy, Ralph really was smart
Santa asked Ralph if he could figure it out
For once Ralph was helpful, he didn't even pout
He really felt needed, he felt good about himself
And from that moment on, Ralph was Santa's main elf

CHRISTMAS WITHOUT MOM

Tis the season to be jolly
There's garland on trees, and plenty of holly
Our family all gathered for our Christmas feast
We bow our heads and pray for world peace
We have turkey, stuffing, and cranberry sauce
It's cozy inside, on the window's there's frost
As we raise our glasses to make a cheer
I realize Christmas is different this year
The food is great, there's presents galore
Our families together, who could ask for more
At that moment I knew it was different this year
Down my cheek, there ran a tear
My mom is in heaven and we miss her so much
She always would have this special touch
But we must carry on, she'd want it that way
She'll be here in spirit, on this Christmas day
Its mom's first Christmas with the angels above
She is now with Jesus, all his glory and love
Though we miss her so much, we have to let go
It's time to release her beautiful soul
So this year at Christmas, though we are apart
Our mom is here, in all our hearts

GRANDMA'S BAND AID

When I was one I took a fall
Grandma put on a band aid, I do recall
It seemed to take away the pain
Grandma could make sunshine out of rain
Grandma's not with us anymore
But I'll never forget band-aids she put on our sores
One day I met this girl and she broke my heart
I should have been smarter right from the start
I wish grandma was here, to make it feel better
My girlfriend just sent me a "Dear John" letter
Could grandma have fixed my "broken" heart?
She did have remedies, she was very smart
Would her band-aid make my heart feel good?
I would put one on if I thought it would
Then one day I found my soul mate
As I look back, it was worth the wait

I now have a son and a beautiful wife
I couldn't ask for much more in my life
Then one day my son joined the service
Going to war made me real nervous
He was very courageous, it was plain to see
He would fight for our country to keep us all free
Then one day my son got shot
I feared the worst, when they didn't say a lot
A few weeks later my son returned
The last two weeks my stomach had churned
He looked real good, though he was pretty sore
We were just happy to have him back from the war
They thought he would die, in the hospital he laid
When he thought of the story of grandma's band aid
He felt grandma there, he noticed a light
At that moment he knew things would be alright

OUR CHRISTMAS CANDLE

While growing up as a little boy
Christmas was always filled with joy
We went to grandmas on Christmas Eve
It was about midnight when we would leave
As we put on our pajamas and got ready for bed
We had visions of sugar plums in our head
Our tree was already in bad condition
But on this night, we had a family tradition
My dad had a candle that he would light
It was mostly red, with a touch of white
I'll never forget the fun we had
As dad told us stories, some happy, some sad
This tradition started many years ago
We would listen to dad as the candle would glow
No matter where we were throughout the year
When dad lit the candle, we'd all gather here
We didn't have much when I was a lad
But we always the stories told by dad
It was many years later, mom and dad passed away
I have a wife, two boys, and a dog called Jay
My brothers and sisters have families of their own
They live far away, so we talk on the phone
We stopped our tradition, many years ago
When I think of memories, my tears would flow
It was Christmas Eve, there was a knock on the door
It was my brother and sister, who I didn't see anymore
They brought us a present this Christmas Eve night
It was mom and dad's candle, what a beautiful sight
It brought back the good times that we all once had
I could feel the presence of mom and dad
From that Christmas on, the candle was lit
And around the Christmas tree we would sit
As we told our stories I could feel the love
I imagine mom and dad smiling from heaven above

THANKS FOR TOMORROW

It's six am, you crawl out of bed
It's a cold winter morning, another day you dread
You put on the coffee, you're barely awake
You take a hot shower, your bones all ache
You want to complain, but who would listen
As you reach from the shower, your towel is missing
At least your coffee finally is done
But going to work is not much fun
You work really hard, eight hours a day
With little respect, and not much pay
As your bills mount up, you see little relief
It's the American way at least that is the belief
You feel you are at the end of your rope
You can't go on, but you know you must cope
Just as you think it can't get any worse
Your car breaks down, you feel you are cursed
But then something happens, that catches your eye
On the news from Iraq, four of our soldiers have died
As tears started running down your cheeks
They show hungry children, so frail and so weak
They tell us of a fire where a whole family would parish
You realize just then, it's your life you should cherish
So you fall to your knees, and ask our Lord above
For another day, with all of his love
From that day on, each morning you pray
The Lord keeps you healthy for another day

GRANDMA'S PURPLE STEW

When life gets tough, and feeling blue
I make some of grandmas purple sew
I find a pot, the biggest one
I make some stew and have some fun
This stew is different, it's one of a kind
It's all mixed together, with purple wine
I love this stew, I must confess
At the fair it was voted the very best
Just throw the ingredients into the huge bowl
Purple stew is good for the soul
I thank my grandma for the recipe she gave
And I promise I'll take it to my grave
It's our family secret that is for sure
Whatever ails you, this is the cure
My favorite part, are the purple tomatoes
It goes just right with the red potatoes
You can stir it for hours, but here is a tip
Throw it in a blender and put it on whip
As the purple stew mixes I sing a tune
Shoobeedoo, shoobeedoo, it will be done real soon
It never comes out, exactly the same
But it belongs in the stew Hall of Fame
I love to share it with my friends
Love and happiness is the message it sends
Many have asked, what's the secret of the stew
But that's our little secret, "I ain't no fool"
Now grandma is in heaven picking purple tomatoes
She's adding some love with purple potatoes

BUCKAROO

When I was young and scrapped my knee
My dad was there to care for me
He'd give me a hug when I was blue
He called me his "Little Buckaroo"
Dad was very protective of me
I was his favorite, everyone could see
He said we'd never be apart
I'd always be in my dad's heart
He taught me to trust in our Lord above
With the Lord in our lives, we'd always have love
Dad got sick seven years ago
Dad had cancer, but you would never know
He never slowed down, he never complained
Though it was clear, dad was in some pain
When my boyfriend asked me to be his wife
I told dad he'd always be the main man in my life
Dad said no matter what I do
I'd always be his "Buckaroo"
I'll never forget dad's huge smile
When I asked him to walk me down the isle
I'll always remember my dad's last day
Before the Lord took dad away
Dad said please don't cry for me
There's no more pain I'm totally free
Dad looked at me, and began to say
Remember our memories every day
When you look towards the sky and the sun shines through
It's me shining down, "Buckaroo"
And when it's gloomy and starts to rain
It's tears of joy, because there is no more pain
So when you think of me, "Please don't feel blue"
Because I am in your heart, "Little Buckaroo"

BUS RIDE TO HEAVEN

We were taking a bus trip out of town
Our bags were packed, we were Georgia bound
Before we arrived at our next stop
People were sleeping, you could hear a pin drop
We were only about a fourth of the way
It looked like it would be a very long day
My wife and I got out to stretch
It was a crisp fall day, some fresh air we would catch
We still had a long journey to go
I'm getting restless, and it began to show
I read a book and magazine
I gazed out the window, what a beautiful scene
I got kind of sleepy, so I took a short nap
I put the book I was reading on my lap
When I woke up I could see it was getting dark
The bus made a stop, in this small park
Everyone was happy, we were almost there
My legs were stiff, but I didn't much care
I looked on over at my wife
She truly was the angel in my life
It was September third, I remember that date
What happened then was truly fate
We were about ten miles from the border
I thought when we arrive, dinner we'd order
Just then I looked up, and saw this bright light
I felt this great crash, it was a horrible sight
Glass was shattering, people were crying
Everywhere you looked things were flying
We never made our destination
Yet I felt at peace, a celebration
The bus finally stopped, the motor stopped revving'
I read this sign," Next stop is heaven"
With my wife on my side, I held her real tight
We're both here in heaven, what a glorious sight
As I stood before Jesus I held his "Good Book"
I thought this was the best trip I ever took

HEADSTONE FOR A CANDLE MAKER

Your life was wax, and you did it well
Until that burning candle fell
We loved the candles that you made
You loved your job, you were well paid
That fire from the candle did you in
But we know you're in heaven, because you had no sins
The candles you left were so cool
And now every year, we light a candle for you

HEADSTONE FOR A FOOTBALL PLAYER

As you lay down beneath the grass
You played your last game, you threw your last pass
You died doing something you loved to do
Too bad that linebacker ran over you
We miss you so much, but we must say goodbye
Now we all hope you're playing up in the sky

HEADSTONE FOR A LIBRARIAN

You were the best librarian I ever have seen
You were smart, witty and a mind so keen
I couldn't feel worse or feel any sadder
When you reached for that book and fell off the ladder
We will all miss you, the children will too
But at least they named the room after you

GOODBYE FOR NOW

When the lord came and got you, there was sorrow and pain
You won't be forgotten, the memories remain
I wish you were with us, this can't really be
You were God's gift to us, how lucky were we
You fought your disease with passion and vigor
You thought not of yourself, no one's heart is bigger
The Lord gave us closure over the years
Our smiles will erase our sorrow and tears
You're now up in heaven, as this earth you depart
But your love you left, is now in our heart

KING OF THE MOUNTAIN

We're all shades of color yellow, white, and black
But it's the love in our hearts, and how we all act
We're all brothers and sisters, no matter our race
We must all work together, on the problems we face
We have no room for bigots, we must all take a stance
If we want all our children to succeed and advance
Mr. King would be proud if he saw us today
But to get to that mountaintop we still have a long way
If we all pull together we have nothing to fear
Just listen to Jesus, his message you'll hear
The Lord really loves us, he's there in our heart
It's the love that he gave us that won't drive us apart
We must preach to our children that we're one human "race"
No matter the color of anyone's face
We've seen all his marches, we've heard people sing
We've all seen his marches, we praise Mr. King
Martin Luther King has died but his "march" must go on
It's time to unite, and together we'll bond
Its forty years later and racism must stop
By now we should be at the "Mountaintop"
So let's all hold hands, and to Jesus we'll pray
That the color of our skin, won't matter some day

BUMPY ROAD

I use to envy the rich and wealthy
But as I get older I'd rather be healthy
Life's never easy, and that's okay
You have to be tough, it gets better each day
Without some detours, on this long winding road
You wouldn't have memories when you grow old
With strength and resilience you will succeed
You'll never be poor, or a person in need
Keep God in your heart, and live a good life
Teach your children respect and love your wife
Never give up, when you feel betrayed
And remember all the friends you have made
When a problem arises do the best that you can
Trials and tribulations will make you a man
Don't ever be afraid, to express your love
And trust in our Lord from heaven above

NO WORRIES

I count my blessings every day
And thank the dear Lord whenever I pray
I'm an upbeat person, don't like to complain
I know there'll be sunshine, after the rain
We all have our problems, I do too
I try not to dwell, it just makes me blue
I try not to worry, I'm pretty laid back
I have my health, there's nothing I lack
When someone has problems, and can't find an answer
I suggest they spend time with a child that has cancer
I really am thankful for food on my table
We may not be rich, but we're healthy and able
When I open my eyes, each glorious day
I just hope during my day things go okay
Dealing with adversity is good for the soul
Helping each other should be our main goal
Sit back and relax, it takes away all your stress
You will feel much better if you try your best
Every day I thank our dear Lord above
And Family and friends, for their guidance and love

BELT

When your pants fall down, I know how you felt
But those days are gone, I am your new belt
I am not cocky but I'll bring you relief
Unlike your suspenders I give you no grief
You can tighten me up or make me real loose
You can count on me, I won't make an excuse
I love your new jeans, I go good with your suits
I'm made of leather, just like your boots
I'm in your closet, just hanging around
I'm the toughest belt, pound for pound
If you get fatter, you can make a new hole
Like your big belly, I'll continue to grow
So don't ever think to replace this old belt
Remember the old days, and how we both felt

ALIVE AND WELL

The alarm went off, I jumped out of bed
I tripped on the dog dish, and fell on my head
I fed my dog, then took a shower
I get dressed, had coffee, and this just takes an hour
When I get to work, it's just my luck
I hit my head on a two wheeler truck
When I left the office, I slammed the door
I jammed my finger, boy was it sore
As I limped around work, people would say
It looks like you're having a terrible day
When I get on the elevator I pressed the third floor
I realized just then we weren't moving any more
Three hours later they came got me out
I'm no complainer, but I started to pout
It was time to go home, I could hardly wait
But my car wouldn't start, I got home real late
When I got home I tripped on my lace
While lying on the floor my dog licked my face
My wife then asked "How was your Day
I'm alive and well, what else could I say

ANGEL BESIDE YOU

There's an angel beside you, I feel in my heart
This angel's been with you right from the start
An angel is sent from heaven above
They are here to protect us, and help spread his love
You can feel their presence, though they can't be seen
It's the warmth in your heart they will bring
An angel's as pure as a white mourning dove
They bring calm and serenity from heaven above
Angels are here, to take worries away
You'll feel peace and tranquility, day after day
When life has you down, and you can't seem to go on
Your angel's beside you, you will feel a bond
It's in your heart where you'll find your real treasure
It's the love you give, is how you'll be measured
Take the hand of your angel, and follow their lead
Go down the right path and there plant your seeds
An angel can only guide you so far
It's the decisions you make that will define who are
So take the Lords teachings and help spread his word
You'll earn your wings, and fly like a bird

MY BONEY CHIROPRACTOR

As I sat in his office all alone
I could feel the pain in every bone
He has a skeleton in this room
It's there for a reason I assume
When the doc walked in he looked so young
At that brief moment, I wish I was done
As he examined me he put me at ease
When he cracked my bones, my pain would cease
As each bone cracked I felt less pain
When he was done, I felt physical gain
I felt so good, I went for a run
And I really felt good, when I was done
I can't wait to see the doctor again
He makes me feel better than anyone can
I miss my bones cracking, it's music to my ears
I get real excited as my appointment nears
When I visit his office, I could hardly move
But later that night I could dance and groove
You can keep your dentist, I'll take my chiropractor
With my back feeling great, I'm the benefactor
So I guess what I'm actually trying to say
Though my teeth won't be fixed, my back is okay

GOOD OLD USA

Buffalo is home of the chicken wing
And Nashville's a place where country stars sing
Orlando's the home for Donald duck
Vegas a place where you try your luck
Cleveland has the Rock and Roll Hall of fame
South Bend has Knute Rockne's Notre Dame
If you love history or major league ball
Come to Boston, see the Sox in the fall
I went to Philadelphia, for some Philly steaks
And in Minnesota are the thousand lakes
Colorado's the most scenic place I've ever been
Pittsburg has the Steelers, and "Blue collar men"
I've been to Palm Beach and walked through the sand
I've been to Chicago, seen the best "Blues" bands
I've seen the flatlands of Kansas City
I've never seen Dallas, and that is a pity
The Seattle rain, the Green Bay cold
I would love to travel each and every road
From Los Angeles to Rhode Island, to Tampa Bay
There's no place more beautiful, than the USA

SAMMY SPIDER

Late September on a cool fall "morn"
In the midst of the grass a spider was born
He had twenty six sisters, thirty nine brothers
But he could care less, because he didn't like others
His name was Sammy, and was really cute
But wherever he went there'd be a dispute
Sammy was smart, and a little mischievous
At times he'd be good, at times he'd be devious
Oh what a web Sammy could spin
Sammy liked trouble and trouble liked him
One early morning, he was up to his tricks
It was Sidney the snake, under some sticks
Sidney was a mean, grouchy old snake
If Sammy pranked him it would be a mistake
Sidney was hungry, he was looking for food
When he saw Sammy he was in a bad mood
We don't know what happened, this is just a hunch
We think Sammy pranked him, then he was Sidney's lunch
No one would ever see Sammy again
His days of tricks had come to an end
Sidney lived a long prosperous life
With his twenty two kids and beautiful wife

GRASS ROOTS

I'm a blade of grass, I am so meek
I'm not real strong, but I'm also not weak
I stay to myself, but I'm not a loner
I tend to complain, but I'm not a moaner
As long as I'm cut at least once a week
I don't ask for much, it's just sunshine I seek
When the wind blows through me, I feel so free
And I love the water from the sprinkler on me
I enjoy the winter, I don't mind the snow blower
The thing that scares me is the blade on the mower
I have a flower who's my best friend
He got cut last week, but he's starting to mend
It's been so dry, I'm turning brown
But I come back greener, this I found
Here comes the sprinkler just in time
Here comes the fertilizer, I hope they got lime
The trees keep it shady, thank God for the leaves
I just hate the fall, it's just one of my peeves
Landscapers have always been great to me
They understand my personality
The other day I saw our number one killer
They're putting in a garden with a rototiller
I'm not complaining, we're all going to die
And someday I may be turf in the sky

BLUE COLLAR TOWN

Steel mills, iron workers, twelve hour shifts
They're your blue collar workers, not your average day stiffs
A beer after work, at the corner bar
They don't drink and drive, because that's not who they are
Blue collar men have very rough hands
And in the back of their trucks you'll find empty cans
Rusted cars in our town you'll see as the norm
Men wear flannel shirts because it is rarely warm
Working two jobs just to make ends meet
They work like dogs so their children can eat
Sunday's the Lords day, a day of rest
It was a time for church, a time to confess
Men were men, there wasn't no doubt
And if dad yelled at you, you didn't dare pout
Mothers stayed home, the dads went to work
Having mom home was a wonderful perk
The world has now changed, for better worse
Woman are working, their careers now come first
While this blue collar town isn't here any more
It's still a great town like it was before

BUFFALO

My toes are frozen, my lips are chapped
My teeth are chattering, thank god they are capped
I cannot move, the snow is deep
My eyes froze shut, I can't even weep
I have cabin fever, I have to get out
If I don't I'll go crazy, there is little doubt
Buffalo I love you, you're my kind of town
But as soon as I thaw I am Florida bound
My house is cold, I feel out of sorts
I'm trading my thermos for flip flop and shorts

PETER PUMPKIN

My name is Peter Pumpkin, and I am really bored
I'm the only pumpkin left, I wish I was a gourd
I know I'm not perfect, I am a little green
If you pick me I'll be orange by the eve of Halloween
I love the kid's costumes, as they all yell "trick or treat"
The bright full moon, simply can't be beat
My friends are gone, they are jack o' lanterns
They sit on a table, their candle slowly burns
I wish someone would pick me off this dreadful vine
I'd make you so proud, and my life would be fine
If you don't pick me I will be okay
I could still be in a pie by Thanksgiving Day

TEQUILA SUNRISE

I just woke up with bloodshot eyes
It's my usual Saturday, Tequila sunrise
I danced, I drank, and partied all night
The girls in their blue jeans, were out of sight
My head is throbbing, there's not much I recall
I hope I did nothing to break the law
I should be all right, in a couple of hours
I still don't know where I got these flowers
That tequila taste is still in my mouth
My best friend today will be my couch
The ringer on my phone, must be turned down
I don't want to hear a single sound
I'm getting flashbacks, of what happened last night
I remember the girl's blue jeans were skin tight
I remember the jukebox, and singing along
To Carrie Underwood's latest song
I swear I'll never drink again
These crazy weekends have to end
I hope someday I do mature
I'm too old for this, that's for sure
It's taking much longer for me to mend
But by Friday night, I do it again
All through the night, I'm not worth a lick
These Tequila, nights are making me sick
But it's the girls in their blue jeans, and a good country song
That makes me feel that's where I belong

I WONDER

I wonder why the sky is blue
Or fish can swim the way they do
I wonder why grass is green
Or the sunset is a beautiful scene
Why do birds fly south each fall?
Why do Redwoods grow so tall?
What keeps stars up in the sky?
Where do birds learn how to fly?
Why do flowers bloom each spring?
With beauty and grace, only flowers can bring
Why are dog's man's best friend?
And when hearts break, how do they mend
You gave us ability, to express our love
Who made the clouds, way up above?
Who gave us feelings, who made our tears?
Who makes us strong, who eases our fears
These questions I hope will be answered some day
I just keep the faith, and continue to pray
Life can be tough, there's times I feel blue
If you ask our Lord, he will pull you through
Just live each day like it could be your last
Because life is fragile and goes to fast
I guess what I'm really trying to say
Is appreciate each and every day

I LOVE NOSTALGIA

Don't look back, some people insist
But I look back and reminisce
I am who I am, and I may not go far
But I believe looking back, helps you know who you are
I'm a baby boomer, but I don't feel old
And I cherish the memories that I hold
I remember watching "Broadway Joe"
He was my hero when I was ten years old
I saw the Beatles, change rock and roll
They came from England many years ago
I remember Woodstock, the hippie generation
And when JFK died, we grieved as a nation
I remember the marches and Martin Luther King
Civil rights he'd preach, and love he would bring
I saw Muhammad Ali, when he was Cassius Clay
He was the greatest boxer, to this very day
Families had each other, they didn't need much more
Our kids were being drafted for the Viet Nam war
I was lucky the war ended when I turned eighteen
The soldiers that fought were the bravest I've seen
I got married, went to work, at age twenty one
The nation was thriving, the war was done
Our world has changed over the years
But I believe love and laughter outweighed the tears

CORINTHIANS II

Forget all the passages, from Corinthians one
Remember in marriage, you must have some fun
Treat everyone great, you must do that first
And always have water to quench your thirst
Study the Corinthians, and you'll always be wise
Think of each other, as winning first prize

WECOME

Everyone's welcome, what ours is yours
We'll listen to problems but promise no cures
Take off your shoes, come on in
Our home is where love and friendship begin
You're welcome for dinner, or just have a beer
You'll feel right at home when you visit here
If its money you want, lets clear the air
We really don't have much money to spare
If it's advice or wisdom you're looking for
I'm not a shrink, so don't ask anymore
Respect my house, my dog and my wife
They're the most precious things I have in my life
We love your company, you are a good friend
We hope you had fun, and please come again

IF YOU SAY.........

If you say I can't I'll say I can
If you tell me never, I'll tell you when
There's no such words in my dictionary
Or any place in my vocabulary
Don't tell me there's something I can't do
I wasn't born yesterday, mama raised no fool
I may not be the sharpest tool in the shed
But one thing I do is use my head
I have common sense, I always was street smart
I am no Di Vinci, but I am a piece of art
Don't put me down, because I will rise up
I can be a vicious dog, or be a loving pup
Don't corner me, I am like an old dirty rat
I'll come out fighting, but you must know that
I like a challenge that is for sure
If you show me a sickness, I'll show you a cure
With age comes wisdom, and with that be told
Don't think I'm weak, because I am old
My math skills are good, my memories great
I might go to college, it's never too late
I have some gray, throughout my hair
But I'm a loving person, and truly do care
So excuse me if I sound ruthless and rude
Don't patronize me, I'm not in the mood

SWEET POTATO TENNESEE

It's a Saturday night, there was a star filled sky
And Mama was cooking sweet potato pie
As we sit on the porch, by the light of the moon
We listened to an old Johnny Cash tune
Uncle Bob might come over and play his guitar
If he isn't honky Tonkin down at the town bar
Papa would play spoons, and we'd all sing along
Most of the time it was an old country song
There were times we would sing, 'til the wee of the morning
It was lots of fun, it never gets boring
Country life was just fine for us
Life was simple, rarely a fuss
Sunday morning Pa and I would go fish for perch
We were home by ten to go to church
Our town was small, we knew everyone
We had a county fair that was so much fun
We might be country bumpkins, but we do love our great city
We are pretty smart, and we really can be witty
If I live there forever, that's all right with me
Because there's no other place I'd rather be
Smelling grits in the morning and apple pie at night
I felt secure, and knew everything would be right
When I went to bed at night I always would pray
That my life would always be this way

HEADSTONE FOR A MARRIAGE COUNSELOR

You listened to problems all day long
You helped many couples when their marriage went wrong
You never took sides, you spoke from the heart
And couples were happy went they would depart
You were very honest, you told them no lies
That probably led to your early demise
When you told that poor guy to leave his mean wife
She pulled out her gun and ended your life
How times seem to fly, it's been a year you were buried
But in heaven you're happy because nobody's married

HEADSTONE FOR A TRAFFIC COP

Other cops, they fought crime
Yet you worked hard all the time
You could have used a little luck
You never seen that pickup truck
You were well respected among your peers
And to everyone you eased their fears
Traffic will never be the same
And no one will ever achieve your fame
You did it all with style and grace
And now up in heaven it's a much safer place

HEADSTONE FOR A CLOWN

You made us all laugh, the kids love you so
You were the hit of the circus, as you put on a show
I'll never forget when I sat in my seat
The elephant crushing you under his feet
I know you're in heaven, because you don't have a sin
As they picked you up you still had your grin

HEADSTONE FOR A CANDY MAKER

You made the best candy, we knew you'd go far
Your name was on a wrapper of a candy bar
You made your great candy, from morning to night
Then you sat there and ate until your very last bite
You ate until you died, that's what they say
What did you in was that last Milky Way
We just hope with all the candy you ate
You can get in to St. Peters gate

HEADSTONE FOR A DRUNKEN SAILOR

Ye was the best sailor who sailed the sea
You were rarely sober your life was care free
The story has it you lost a bet
You were the biggest welcher that anyone met
They say someone threw you over the ship
I just hope from your rum you got a last sip
If I know you, you put up a good fight
Unfortunately the sharks were hungry that night

WAKE UP

Wake up little baby, do not cry
It's already morning, wipe the sleep from your eye
You have things to explore, so much to learn
The things you get, you will have to earn
Don't get disheartened, aim high not low
Keep your sweetness and youth when you grow old

HEADSTONE FOR A FLOOR CLEANER

You buffed those floors, you made them shine
A more experienced stripper you'll never find
All the walking you did kept you fit and lean
You were the hardest worker we've ever seen
There was nobody better, you were the best
When the machine ran you over it made quite a mess
We're all very sad, it's so hard to cope
Now all that is left is your bucket of soap

HEADSTONE FOR A ZOOKEEPER

You were the monkey's best friend, they felt a connection
You gave them your love and lots of affection
Everyone loved you, you couldn't be beat
Though the bears looked at you like a piece of meat
You spent all your spare time at the zoo
We all knew where to call if we needed you
But now we're all sad, we can't stop crying
Since you were the entrée for that mountain lion
They say they will name the cub after you
But it won't be the same at the city zoo

HEADSTONE FOR A CEMENT MIXER

You were the best mixer, you were much respected
But what happened next wasn't expected
You slipped and fell into the mixer
You're now part of the driveway, a permanent fixture

LIFES IMAGES FROM A DEAF AND BLIND MAN

I can't see my son or darling wife
But I love them so much, they are my whole life
I'm deaf and blind, I've been so since birth
I take nothing for granted, I know what life's worth
I never heard a cricket in the park
I've never seen stars, when the sky was dark
But I know Jesus loves me, it's his voice I hear
And I can see Virgin Mary, it's a vision so clear
Someday I'll be in heaven by the Lords side
But for now I'll enjoy life and all the treasures I find

A PICKLE IN A JAR

I am just a pickle in a pickle jar
Life is pretty boring, I can't go very far
I am a juicy dill, I wish that I was sweet
Someday a cute dill pickle I hope that I do meet
I was a big cucumber, so vibrant and so green
I was so very healthy, I was fit and very lean
I sound like I'm complaining, but life's been pretty neat
I feel like I was lucky, I wasn't born a beet
The story that I tell you, I don't need to embellish
And someday if I'm lucky I'll end up in a relish
I tell my pickle friends how lucky that we are
And someday soon we'll meet in a salad bar
But for now I'll wish and dream that hopefully some day
I find my one and only on a veggie relish tray

SAMMY SNOWBLOWER

I am your best friend, I'm always true blue
I give you my best, I'm here to serve you
You have to admit I'm well worth the price
I get you through snow, the slush and the ice
Someday I'll retire, I'll lay in the sun
But until that day my job is not done
My job is exciting, it never gets boring
I'm the first thing you see, each cold winter morning
When you put me away and bring out your mower
Don't forget about me, I'm your trusty snow blower

IRISH PARADISE

In South Buffalo you don't need a car
You can walk to your favorite Irish bar
They love Notre Dame, if you don't it's a sin
The Irish all treat you like you were kin
There's a catholic church on every block
We pray in the morning, and at night we rock
There's a funeral home a stone's throw away
If you like Irish food, it's a great place to stay
We don't lock our doors, there's very little crime
Everyone's having a very good time
We have the cutest lassies you've ever seen
It's always St. Patty's day everything is green
Everyone's name seems to be 'O Brian
If you're not drunk, you're probably not trying
If you're not Irish living here could be risky
But everyone's happy drinking Irish whiskey
As Irish eyes are smiling, you're never too old
It's here you could find your big pot of gold

FLY LIKE A BIRD

This might sound strange or a little absurd
But if I could come back, I'd come back as a bird
I would fly through the sky on a bright sunny day
I'd need a GPS so I don't lose my way
From the great Rocky Mountains to the ocean so blue
I'd fly during the day and night time too
All my food would basically be free
And I could spend hours up in a tree
I'd go south for the winter, and never see snow
I could fly high or I could fly low
To see the world from way up above
It's something I'd treasure and truly love
I'd feel so alive and totally free
There would be no place I'd rather be
I could fly by a lake, take a bath in a pond
Find a cushy roof I could safely land on
I'd have no debt or bills to pay
I'd never be tired at the end of the day
I'd fly over cities and each little town
I'd always be up, I'd never be down
No more cancer and all the sorrow
I'd just live for today, not worry about tomorrow

SOMEDAY DAD

Dad like you I want be smart
And like you dad I want a big heart
I'd like to be a football star
I'd like to be rich, own a nice car
"Son you are young yet very astute
You're charming, witty and very cute
Make intelligent decisions and always be kind
Get a good education, develop your mind"
Someday dad I'd like to teach
I have many goals I hope I can reach
I'd like to feed the hungry and clothe the poor
Maybe study about cancer and help find a cure
You're my mentor, my hero and always will be
All the values in life that you taught me
"Son someday when you are a man
You'll realize then I was your biggest fan
I tried to be a good father to you
I'm amazed how fast you matured and grew
I wish your mother could see you today
In Heaven I hope to see her someday"
Dad, each night I keep mom in my prayers
In my heart I feel her and I know she still cares
In my journey through life you showed me the way
You taught me to embrace each coming day
In Heaven someday with Mom you will be
Until then I say thanks for being here for me

ME VS LEUKEMIA

It's a twelve round fight and it's about to begin
Don't bet against me I'm gonna win
It's the fight of my life I had no time to train
I'm as tough as nails you won't hear me complain
Ill beat you leukemia just you wait and see
You've never seen anyone quite like me
I'll come out swinging I won't go down
There's something inside me I have found
The persistence to take all the pain you dish out
I have inner strength you won't see me pout
It's not only me that I'm fighting for
I have family friends and so much more
You might think you're stronger and smarter than me
But I'll win the fight and be cancer free
You can break my spirit I'll keep fighting back
You can see that its confidence I do not lack
I'll jab and duck then throw you a right hook
You'll pay for the chemo and meds I took
You may think I'm cocky but you started this fight
You didn't fight fair it just wasn't right
I do not fear you, you fight dirty for sure
Someday you'll see they will find a cure
But until that day comes don't think you have won
We'll attack you each day this fight just begun
The needles the meds the hospital stays
The sleepless nights the grueling days
Give me your best shot I'm taking you down
I'm the toughest foe you ever found
You caused lots of heartache over the years
You hurt many families turning laughter to tears
With the help of our doctors you'll go down for the count
There's no doubt in my mind we will knock you out
It's now round twelve they just rang the bell
And all that is left are the stories I tell
Leukemia will be a word from the past
And I'll be happy to say "you are gone at last"
**Dedicated to Emily Borodzik and her family who
are courageously fighting leukemia**

JOEY'S LETTER

Getting older is no easy thing
Lately I feel every little ding
I wake up each morning with a different ache
Each mile I run is harder to make
I could complain but who would hear
Growing old is my biggest fear
Just when I thought I had no answer
I helped at a benefit for children with cancer
At this beautiful gala, wealthy people attended
It was a magical night that I wished never ended
There was glitz, and glamour, tuxes and gowns
There was lots of laughter no time for frowns
That night I worked hard as a volunteer
It was for Camp Good Days, whom I hold so dear
I worked as a counselor for the kids
While others worked auctions and had to take bids
The kids all had fun and the gala went on
These kids have cancer they all have a strong bond
I spent some time with this boy named Joe
He's a very cute boy, he's 8 years old
Just watching this courageous young boy smile
Made me forget my problems for a little while
Working for camp always makes me feel better
But what really hit home was "Joey's letter"
He was about to read it up on the stage
He asked if I'd read it as he handed me the page
It read, Dear Lord I have cancer my name is Joe
I'm telling you things you probably know
I have a great life a great mom and dad
But as I look in their eyes they look really sad
I make sure I pray to you every night
And I know with you Jesus I will be alright
I only have one more thing to pray
Make mom and dad happy and show them the way
Signed Joey
From the moment on I felt much better
And it was because of Joey's letter

"Joey is always will be an inspiration in my life endeavors"

DEJAVU

You felt you were down that road before
And somehow you knew who would knock at your door
Faces in the crowd you never saw
But something about them you do recall
You travel somewhere far, far away
And you felt you were there on a previous day
You have a dream of a distant place
And in your dream is a familiar face
Could you have lived a previous life?
Could you have been there with your wife?
Could you have been a brave young soldier?
Do you ever think you could be much older?
Could you have sailed the ocean blue
Could you have been with Columbus' crew?
You could have been a pilgrim on the Mayflower
You could have seen Hitler when he was in power
Flashbacks can tell you where you were before
At times you wish you could remember more
You might have been a part of history
But everything seems to be a mystery
Were you Madam Currie did you find a cure
There's nothing you really know for sure
You could have been alive during the pioneer days
You might have liked the simpler ways
You could have been an author or great composer
Maybe someday we will all have closure
Is it possible we all control our fate?
Whatever it is we will have to wait

WALK IN THEIR SHOES

Imagine walking in someone else's shoes
If you did you'd be singing the blues
You see the fireman cleaning his truck
But surviving a fire isn't just luck
It takes months of training to go in that house
Would they ever again see their kids or their spouse?
The bravery it takes we do not know
The stress in their life it takes a toll
A garbage man is an unlikely hero
But they're out there when it's ten below zero
The highway men who salt our street
All the snow they remove and the ice and sleet
Doctors and nurses they get good pay
But they make a commitment day after day
I respect teachers no matter the grade
I also respect the teacher's aide
Construction workers climb without fear
They live a hard life that's pretty clear
Our crossing guards with our children we trust
The way people drive they are a must
When our favorite team happens to lose
Stop and think if you could fill their shoes
To our soldiers, I would like to say
We're proud of you and for you we pray
When I think of your ultimate sacrifice,
You're very brave and as cool as ice
As you're stationed in Iran or Iraq,
I pray every soldier does come back
No more wars, no more guns,
We can't afford to lose more daughters or sons
Children with cancer who are terminally ill
These are shoes I pray won't be filled
But when a child dies in heaven he'll be
My tears are so much I can hardly see
As I pray for our heroes and a child that's ill
I realize the Lord's shoes could never be filled

PATCHES THE FROG

Patches was shy a little bit meek
He lived on a lily pad out on a creek
He was your typical frog he loved to eat flies
But they were hard to catch because he had but one eye
He didn't have friends and that made him sad
He just sat around on his green lily pad
The other little frogs would play all day long
But poor little Patches felt he didn't belong
With a patch on his eye he didn't look the same
And he never got asked to play Froggy games
He sat there each day watching other young frogs
They were all having fun jumping on and off logs
Patches wished he could join in the fun
He'd watch all day long until they were done
Why do they treat me the way that they do
I have but one eye, but I am a frog too
Each night before bed his mom wiped his tears
She'd read him a story then eased all his fears
She told him don't worry someday you will see
When you meet a new friend so happy you'll be
One day Patches saw this poor helpless frog
He went under water when he fell off a log
The little frog panicked because he couldn't swim
Patches thought quickly he threw him a limb
From that day on he had a good friend
And Patches would never be lonely again

**THE MORAL OF THE STORY IS JUST BECAUSE SOMEONE'S
DIFFERENT, THEY'RE LIKE ME AND YOU
THEY DO HAVE A HEART AND THEY HAVE FEELINGS TOO**

FLIGHT 3407-NOT FORGOTTEN

How our lives have all changed these past 2 years
It's painful to see through our heartache and tears
Only time will heal our still broken hearts
Life must go on but where do we start
Each day that goes by there's a little less pain
We have to believe this wasn't in vain
We remember the good times though you're with us no longer
It's hard to believe this made us all stronger
We have pictures, home movies we'll never forget
The good time we shared the places we went
We struggle each hour of each waking day
We look for some answers each night when we pray
With the strength of our lord, we'll try to get through
We'll fight for flight safety there's so much to do
We'll fight politician's bureaucracy and such
We won't rest a day because we love you so much
Sitting by your lord's side you must feel so proud
Through our books and our poems our voices ring loud
By now they must know we won't go away
There'll be new regulations for safety some day
When we look to the skies with the stars up above
We know you are there we feel all your love
Our families are growing, we've made some new friends
This helps us get by as our heart someday mends

Our children & grandchildren will all know of you
We'll share stories with friends and our memories too
So keep smiling from heaven till we see you some day
Know your legacy lives on and in our hearts you will stay

A FAIRY "TAIL" WEDDING

Once upon a time in this big old house
Lived a rabbit and a grouchy old mouse
The rabbit was cool beyond compare
And he had the finest light brown hair
One day this rabbit met this mouse
He said some day you'll be my spouse
The mouse looked shocked as she ran away
She said "you'll never see that day"
Well it just so happened this rabbit was rich
As he tried to make one last pitch
The mouse was really taken back
But it wasn't confidence this rabbit lacked
"I'll marry you on one condition
Our bedroom has a large petition
You stay on the left, I'll stay on the right
We'll always stay happy, we'll never fight
The rabbit thought Oh what the heck
With that he gave her a little peck
The wedding was large, the guests got along
There was music, drinks, dancing and song
At the end of the evening they cut the cake
There was a piece for everyone there to take
It was a fairy "tail" wedding from beginning to end
Everyone danced family and friend
So off on their honeymoon they did go
And they lived happily ever after as far as we know!

TEARS OF A CLOWN

It's a smile you'll see, never a frown
Tears of joy not tears of a clown
Everyone thinks I'm happy & jolly
I never let on that I'm melancholy
Making others laugh is what I do best
But sometimes I hurt I must confess
I never complain, what good would it do
I'm only human and my heart breaks too
I know some day I will find my mate
I'm a romantic who truly believes in fate
For my good health I thank our Lord
My mind is as sharp as a double edges sword
I'm an everyday guy from a blue collar town
There's no time for pity, or getting down
We're only on earth for a very short time
And I still have many mountains to climb
Gloom & doom aren't in my book
The joy in my heart is where I look
I may be poor and down on my luck
I may be down to my last buck
But you won't see a tear running down my cheek
Go somewhere else if it's a sorrow you seek
The lord put me here for a reason I'm sure
My intentions are good my heart is pure
I make grownups laugh and babies smile
I try to go that extra mile
The lord has given me a special gift
I give people who are down a little lift
I pray to our lord almost every night
I live a good life with my future in sight
I'll never give up and I won't wear a frown
From me you won't see the "Tears of a clown"!

IT'S NICE GROWING OLD

Our world is changing that's what I'm told
But I'm here to declare it's nice growing old
You now are retired, you can sleep to noon
You can sit out at night by the silvery moon
You have no more schedules you're finished with school
You no longer follow the golden rule
You can eat sweets, your teeth won't get sore
With dentures your teeth don't hurt any more
If you are bored you pretend you can't hear
Your eyesight is fading but with glasses they're clear
You have short term memory but you remember your past
You swim and you jog though not quite as fast
You're aging real slow like a fine wine
And you do get a discount whenever you dine
Each morning you wake you have a new pain
But nobody cares so why even complain
Your new best friend is now Viagra
It will make you feel like the mighty Niagara
But let's be honest, you've seen your best day
But with that being said, you did it your way!

SEPTEMBER 11TH

It was September 11th two thousand one
Nothing seemed different as our work day begun
We were at work for only a couple of hours
When someone said a jet hit the twin towers
We listened to the radio we had no TV
But we didn't need pictures of these images to see
One twin tower was all fire and smoke
We tried to understand as the president spoke
Just then a jet hit the other twin tower
We know this was war, within a few hours
People were jumping out of windows of fire
Our firemen & policemen you'd have to admire
Our pentagon was now under attack
All you could see was the smoke so black
A jet went down in a Pennsylvania field
The passengers on the jet refused to yield
They were all heroes they refused to give in
They had a plan, but they couldn't win
The passengers on flight ninety- three
Gave their lives so we could stay free
It's what heroes are made of imagine their plight
They fought these terrorists with all their might
It's been 8 years and we still feel the pain
How could these terrorists be this insane?
We should all close our eyes and go back to that day
When this radical group tried taking our freedom away
We are stronger and closer than we've ever been
We must never forget, as we all slowly mend

SEPTEMBER 11TH-A DAY OF AWAKENING

It's the 6th anniversary of September 11th
We pray for the brave souls that went to heaven
I'll never forget that dark gloomy day
What a horrible price we all had to pay
American's thought they've seen everything
But nobody expected what this day would bring
America came together, we were united
When our anthem was played, we all got excited
People hung flags and wore red white and blue
And over our stadiums our fighter jets flew
Our firemen and policemen were at ground zero
Everyone there was America's hero
Our family & friend seemed closer than ever
And our patriotism has never been better
We can't get complacent we must continue to pray
Remember those brave souls who vanished that day
That day was horrific, be we must always remember
That fateful day the 11th of September
Feel proud to be American we're the land of the free
Thank the troops who protect us they're as brave as could be
And always remember what was done by Bin Laden
As a nation we forgive but it won't be forgotten
When we go about our daily life
Never forget all the grief and strife
Every night we must pray to our dear lord above
But most important don't forget to honor and love

RING OF KNOWLEDGE

Pick up that book turn off that TV
Get wild & adventurous feel totally free
In books you can travel anywhere
You can learn about gems so precious and rare
You'll meet princes & princesses and maybe a king
You'll marvel at the wisdom & knowledge books bring
So, find that book that's just right for you
And experience the world from a different view

DAD'S FOOTPRINTS

It was summer vacation I was 7 years old
My dad just bought me a new fishing pole
Dad knew what I wanted, and this was my wish
To be with my dad when we caught that big fish
Some nights I would sleep with my pole and my net
I'd dream of the big one that dad and I'd get
After our fishing we'd walk in the sand
We'd look for seashells as we walked hand in hand
It wasn't the size of the fish that we caught
It was the fun that we had, and the lessons dad taught
As I walked in dad's footprints on the sand one day
I could tell dad was sad he had something to say
As he looked towards the ocean with a tear in his eye
He said you must remain strong, Dad's going to die
Follow these footprints we made in the sand
Then I'll know you'll grow up to be a good man
Dad passed away early that fall
Being dad's son I walked proud and stool tall
Now with my son we walk in the sand
We follow dad's footprints as we walk hand in hand
It doesn't matter the size of the fish that we caught
It's the love and life's lessons that my dear dad had taught.

GRANDMA'S CHAIR

I can remember at the age of one
Going to gram's was so much fun
I can still picture gram in her red rocking chair
Me on her lap with my brown teddy bear
As she rocked back and forth I'd fall fast asleep
These memories with grandma forever I'll keep
I felt great in grams arms I loved her so much
She made me feel better with her special touch
The lessons she taught the wisdom she gave
Is worth more than money and forever I'll save
It was very sad when grandma grew old
She forgot many stories that she once told
Twenty years later I had kids of my own
Grandma was now in a nursing home
She would still rock in her red rocking chair
And she never let go of my brown teddy bear
I'll never forget it was early September
They said gram went to heaven I'll always remember
I have two great children and a beautiful wife
I have to admit I have a great life
But I wish that my Gram was still here with me
Rocking in her chair like it used to be
Gram may be gone but I still have her chair
I now rock my children with my old teddy bear
Grams now in heaven and we all miss her so
But she'll always be with us wherever we go

BUFFALO, MY FRIEND

Buffalo's my home, my trusty old friend
Hospitality and friendship are feelings you send
Everyone's welcome, you're very diverse
Family traditions always come first
I left my great city of Buffalo
I got tired of winters and three feet of snow
I now live in Florida, the sunshine state
Where lobster and shrimp now fill my plate
I love Buffalo's fish fry's and Canadian beer
The fish we now eat we I catch off the pier
The cold winter mornings, the gray dismal skies
Made leaving for Florida no big surprise
I do miss my family and friends every day
But if you all come down you're welcome to stay
Buffalo I'll always be your number one fan
But instead of windburn, I now have a tan
I spread your good name all over Palm Coast
Your cultures and arts are what I miss most
Though we settled in Florida and we are far apart
Buffalo you'll always be here in our hearts

NOTHING TO SAY

Believe or not I have nothing to say
I'll think about nothing the rest of the day
Nothing is happening I am really bored
I now draw a blank where my thoughts were once stored
My life is good, I'm not complaining.
I just don't care if it's sunny or raining
I don't even care if there's snow on the ground
I don't care if it's quiet or loud
I've cleansed my soul my mind is clear
if I have nothing to say there's nothing to fear
For the first time I'm finally at peace
Worrying in life is what I like least
There's no more pressure no expectations
My life is now like a summer vacation
I have no opinions but this I will share
If I can't control it, I don't really care
Life is too short, live and let live
The older I get, the more I should give
Now that I'm silent I listen a lot
I appreciate more the things that I got
Goodbye to the clouds hello to the sun
Take time to relax and just have some fun
My body is toned, my heart beats strong
Serenity is here my troubles long gone

MY LUCKY CHARM

I'm drinking green beer I don't see the harm
I'm 1200 miles from my lucky charm
I may not be Irish but it's St. Patty's day
I wish I was with you somehow someway
You're my cute leprechaun, you're my pot of gold
I love you till I'm one hundred years old
You smell like a rose you're my 4-leaf clover
I'll tell you I miss you over and over
Will you wear my shamrock its light Kelly green?
It's for the prettiest lassie I've ever seen
I'm the happiest laddie when you are with me
I love your blue eyes and the beauty they see
At the end of rainbow way up in the sky
It reminds me of you as the bluebirds fly by
I've never seen a leprechaun but I'm one lucky man
The day I met you my new life began
Today we're all Irish and from this laddie to you
I'll drink a green beer and think only of you
We're one lucky couple though we are miles apart
Today is St. Patty's day and you're here in my heart

CHILL FACTOR

The weather man says it's very cold
Please tell me something I already don't know
He says stay inside it's 10 below zero
Of course, I'll stay in because I am no hero
I turn up the heat, but I still see my breath
I feel we're all on the brink of death
I must go out and shovel some snow
It looks like we have three feet or so
When I go outside, I'm too cold to move
I shovel slow, I have nothing to prove
My eyes are frozen, I can't feel my toes
I can't even blink cause my eyes won't close
I wish that I could go back inside
Why is my driveway so long and so wide?
This is no way to live if you have a weak heart
The birds fly south they are very smart
I must buy salt to melt all the ice
It's worth all the money no matter the price
I'm not a genius but this I do know
I'd rather be somewhere where there is no snow
I go in the house I turn up the heat
Sit in my chair and put up my feet
I turn on the weather to see what's in store
As the weather man smiles, the temperatures four
That is a good temperature for a polar bear
It's got to be sunny and eighty somewhere
How much of this can we all take?
My skin is so dry and my bones all ache
Shouldn't we all be out in the sun
Enjoying the warmth and having some fun
I turn off the weather I had enough
Getting through winter is going to be tough
As I sit in the house with my girlfriend and dog
I dream about summer and put on a log

OUR FALLEN SOLDIER

One day my boy came up to me
He said dad someday a soldier I'll be
I hugged him and gave him all my love
I told him I'd pray to the dear lord above
He brushed his teeth and went to bed
And I'll never forget the words he said
Dear Jesus, I'm only 10 years old
You are my savior in the bible I'm told
I want to fight for our freedom someday
Every night that's the first thing I ask when I pray
Whatever you tell me is what I will do
But know that I bleed red white and blue
My tears were falling they were pouring out
I was proud of my little boy scout
As the years flew by and my son turned eighteen
He was a smart young man so tall and so lean
One day he asked if he could talk to me
He is my little boy and he always will be
He said dad I want to fight in Iraq
He said please don't worry I will come back
I was sad yet proud and I held back my tears
I told him I loved him
I didn't mention my fears
The day he left and boarded his plane
My heart was breaking I could feel the pain
Then came that faithful hot summer day
My son sent a letter and this it did say
Dear mom and dad if you're reading this letter
I wish I could hug you and make you feel better
My dear lord took my rifle today
I'm now up in heaven and it's here I will stay
I love you mom and I love you dad
I didn't die in vain so don't be sad
As I sit here by Jesus and I put down my gun
I'll always be proud that I was your son

THE OLD FISHERMAN

My wife just left, and took all I had
She took my dog, I'm lonely and sad
I have no car, it was repossessed
I'm tired and weary, I need some rest
I'm a little confused, I can't think straight
Sometimes I wonder, what is my fate
It can't get much worse, my life is a mess
I'm a church going guy, with a lot to confess
My problems are many, how much can I take
I wish some mornings I wouldn't awake
It was a Saturday morning, the clouds were gray
The way I felt, it was the perfect day
I drove to a place called Stoney point ridge
It was there I'd jump off Stoney point bridge
When I got to this bridge there was this old man
He said sit down, you need not stand
He told me how fishing took his worries away
Fishing could brighten his darkest days
He told me a story, he was at the end of his rope
He had little to live for, it was so hard to cope
His savings was lost, life looked bleak
He was about to jump in Stoney point creek
Just then he heard this little boy yell
From the slippery banks this young boy fell
He jumped in the creek to save this young boy
From that moment on all he felt was joy
He said he knew that this was God's way
And now his life would be okay
I felt much better as I wiped my tears
And I never forgot him over the years
I never saw this old man again
But I knew my new life would now begin

KEVIN EVERETT, ON THE LORDS TEAM

As the clock ticked down to its final tick
The Broncos lined up for the winning kick
I had this bad feeling, things weren't going our way
It was an emotional roller coaster most of the day
With zero seconds on the clock the ball went through
The Bills had just lost, and we all felt blue
The fans felt cheated, there was disbelief
They stole the ballgame just like a thief
As I sat in my seat, I could not move
Our team played tough, they had something to prove
The stadium was emptying, it was a somber crowd
Just two hours earlier fans were excited and loud
I felt the Bills pain and I felt the stress
As I sat in the stadium, I began to regress
Earlier in the game I do recall
Kevin Everett hit a Bronco, who was carrying the ball
He didn't get up, the players looked scared
The instant replay had just been aired
We all felt helpless, my eyes filled with tears
All I saw on fans faces were their concerns and their fears
A silver lining, I was trying to find
That hit on Kevin Everett kept entering my mind
I just sat there for an hour praying to our lord
Just then there was a vision on our large scoreboard
As I looked at our scoreboard, I heard this voice say
"Son I know this was an emotional day
With Kevin's faith he will walk again
His life is not over, it's about to begin
Kevin is special, a quality tight end
But instead of playing football it's my word he will spread
His love for our Lord will never again waiver
Kevin will teach us that Jesus is our Savior"

FROM PILOT CONTROL

FLIGHT 3407

This is pilot control, flight 3407
The weather looks fine as we now enter heaven
We had a safe flight though we did come in late
When we depart from the plane, there's St. Peters gate
The lord just informed us of prayers sent to heaven
They were sent by the loved ones on flight 3407
We took a small detour but there's nothing to fear
The lord will make sure we're all safe up here
We see churches full as loved ones say their goodbyes
We see sadness and tears in everyone's eyes
To each mother, father husband or wife
"be happy for us, go on with your life
Though we're no longer with you we'll never be apart
If the memories are still in your heart
That's our gift to you as our lord shows the way
He assures us we'll all be together some day
Our legacy lives in each one of you
Encourage our children in whatever they do
Put on your best smile and don't get depressed
We're with our lord Jesus, our sins all confessed
It's amazing up here, there's no wind or ice
There's a beautiful garden in paradise
There's so much to tell you but there is this one thing
Please remember us in worship and whenever you sing
Know we're always thinking of you
And know we're beside you in whatever you do
Though it's time to sign off from flight 3407
Remember us always, we'll be smiling from heaven"

**DEDICATED TO THE PASSENGERS AND
LOVED ONES FROM FLIGHT 3407**

MY HEART

Whenever I'm scared or feeling blue
I look in my heart ask what to do
I'm very confused and don't know where to start
The best friend I have is my trusty old heart
Your advice is free, and it makes me feel better
It can let you forget that dear john letter
Your heart is where all your answers lie
It will never leave you as your years fly by
Your heart does get broken, but it always mends
It's always quite clear with the message it sends
When you are hurting your heart hurts too
When you feel sad your heart feels blue
Your heart will tell you when it's time to leave
It will tell you whose lying and who to believe
Trust your brain but feel your heart
It's the last thing that beats before you depart
A faithful companion right to the end
It's your mentor, your conscience and your best friend
People with heart are easy to spot
They live, they love and laugh a lot
So, thank you heart, I do need you so
You're here when we're high, you're here when we're low

SERENITY

Take a step back and just take a breath
Every little problem isn't life or death
Problems you have will go away
Tomorrow will be a better day
Relax and let things take its course
Your inner spirit is a mighty force
Sort things out and clear your mind
You can deal with problems of any kind
Sometimes you need to get away
Take a walk on the beach on a sunny day
Get away from the hustle and bustle of the city
Some people are stressed, it's really a pity
Meditation is soothing to the mind
Inner peace is what you need to find
Don't let anyone bring you down
Put on your great smile, remove that frown
Stay positive and forget all negativity
Only then you will have peace and serenity
Serenity will conquer all your fears
There'll be no anger, no more tears
Only then will you find out who you are
Happiness in your life won't seem so far
These mountains you climb won't seem so high
You can do anything if you try
The world is chaotic but if you are serene
Your soul will be cleansed, you'll feel refreshed and clean
Serenity is a very good feeling
When you find it, you'll start the process of healing
With peace and serenity, you'll enjoy every day
And with our lord in your life you'll now find your way

AN EASTER "TAIL"

I took a walk in the park two days before Easter
I slipped on some ice and fell right on my keester
As I lay on the ground, I couldn't help but think
I'll be sore for Easter and that would stink
I tried to get up, but I hurt my knee
So, I crawled on over and sat by this tree
It wasn't that cold so by this tree I would I sit
Figuring someone would come by in a little bit
I tried to walk but it was quite a battle
Just then I noticed this large dark shadow
As I called for some help all I could see
Was this strange looking bunny behind this huge tree
He looked friendly, he didn't show fear
But as I looked in his eyes, I noticed a tear
What happened next you may think I'm crazy
But at the time it didn't really faze me
The white furry rabbit said to me
"I'm very depressed, as sad as can be
He told his story, which wasn't too funny
By now I guessed he was the Easter bunny
He said over the years he'd been all but forgotten
As I saw his sorrow, I said that's really rotten
He said kids loved Santa, he brings them toys
Christmas is great for little girls and boys
I know I'm no Santa, I am no fool
But I love kids and have feelings too
As I sat on this stump and gave my knee a rest
I told him I always liked him the best
When I get back home this may sound insane
But I'm going to start an Easter bunny campaign
He was so impressed he jumped for joy
He thought about every little girl and boy
As I shook his paw I said "have no fear"
You will be popular by early next year
The rest is history and as I end this "tail"
The Easter bunny then hopped down the bunny trail

TIME WASTED

It's not time wasted, it's just wasted time
The time in a bottle, it's yours and it's mine
I learned years ago it's not the time that we had
It's making that time happy or sad
How cool would it be if time could stand still?
I really believe someday that it will
We're all in a hurry for what I don't know
We must enjoy life before we grow old
Live each second, each minute, of each waking day
Don't worry about tomorrow, it will all be okay
There's a time in my childhood I'd like to have back
It's time I had wasted, not time that I lacked
Live for today, don't look far ahead
Don't wish for tomorrow, that's what my dad said
I yearned for the day I turned sixteen
I would be a man, if you know what I mean
Life is short, so enjoy every day
Live all your dreams along the way
Enjoy your life wherever you are
Take time to explore, reach for the stars
There's only so many Christmas's so we must remember
Don't worry about winter when it's only September
Our time will come when god takes us away
Don't worry about this, you'll won't know the day
Remember the good times, that's what we should do
Time doesn't stand still for me or for you
Tomorrows not promised nor should it be
Smell the green grass, climb that oak tree
Take a swim in the ocean' go fish in that pond
Give someone a hug, you will feel a bond
Last but not least thank our lord up above
He fills all our hearts with passion and love

TIS THE SEASON

Ho ho ho, gee whiz, gee golly
Tis the season to be jolly
You put up your tree, hang stockings with care
There's a feeling of Christmas in the air
You're all stressed out, you're falling to pieces
You still need to get gifts for your nephews and nieces
As your bills pile up and can't get paid
The feeling of Christmas soon will fade
Visiting people, you don't even know
Driving your car through the ice and snow
Relatives saying what you bought them don't fit
I guess that is something I'll never get
Someone has to dress up as Santa Claus
It's hard when the suit looks like a lost cause
My girlfriend asks me why do I drink
I tell her Christmas puts me over the brink
I may get drunk but that's just me
The more I drink the better I'll be
The true meaning of Christmas I can't find anymore
It's less about Jesus, it's more shopping at stores
The Santa at the mall even looks kind of crabby
As I eat Christmas snacks, I feel kind of flabby
But you say it's all about being together
I think it's more about the terrible weather
Every Christmas brings me another tear
I pray I'm in Tampa for Christmas next year
I'll take the white sand over this slush
I'll take walking the beach and no more rush
It looks nice at Christmas but on the other hand
I wouldn't mind sitting in the hot white sand
Just think how much fun Christmas could be
Sipping a rum and coke under a palm tree
Next year when I'm out of sorts
I want a ticket out of town instead of shorts

OUR GENERATION

Generation after generation
Times have changed in our great nation
Like the sand pouring in an hour glass
The years flew by way to fast
The sixties don't seem so long ago
When we saw this young band on the Sullivan show
They were four young lads from Liverpool
They were our new heart throbs, they were very cool
King had a "dream" that we'd all be one "race"
Kennedy sent rockets into outer space
You could park for free in a parking lot
And flower children were smoking pot
Sandals and bell bottoms are what the kids wore
As college students protested the Viet name war
The seventies came and the war was ending
Peace was the message our young kids were sending
As the turmoil ended there was a breath of fresh air
The peace movement stopped, and protests were rare
There was racial equality and integration
Everyone now got a good education
Politics would never be the same
As Watergate put our nation to shame
People were working and prices were down
The disco was the new craze in town
The boys were wearing flowered shirts
Girls looked great in their mini skirts
Our moms wore dresses, they really looked cute
And our dads they wore their leisure suits
The eighties came and they changed our ways
Factories were closing every day
The nineties came and we went high tech
Computers would have a lasting effect
Computers would change the human race
Our world was moving at a much faster pace
We had cell phones, surround sound and DVDs
We had electronic devices on our keys
History should make us all smarter some day
And hopefully our wisdom will show our children the way

PREACHING TO THE CHOIR

A man once asked if I had a dollar to spare
I didn't but instead I sent him a prayer
You are a proud man and for this I admire
Don't be ashamed you're preaching to the choir
A family in church took up a whole pew
When the collection plate came, they passed it on through
The father looked embarrassed, his kids poorly dressed
I don't have a dime the father confessed
Bringing your kids to church, though your money expired
We give when we can, you're preaching to the choir
Last week in the park a girl sat there crying
If I said I wasn't curious you'd know I'd be lying
I asked this sweet girl why she was sad
She said last month we buried my dad
She said she felt like her heart was on fire
I said I lost my dad, you're preaching to the choir
As I took my dog for his daily walk
I noticed my neighbor and went over to talk
As he petted my dog, he started to cry
He said he had a dog, and last week he had died
As a child my dog got hit by a car
I loved him so much, so I know how you are
A love for your dog you have to admire
But your heart will mend, you're preaching to the choir
My 25th marathon I ran yesterday
I saw this girl fall, on the street she did lay
I helped her up, we had one more mile
I told her she'd make it and she gave me a smile
To finish a marathon, she ran wire to wire
I fell many times, you're preaching to the choir
At the ripe old age of eighty-seven
I passed away and was up in heaven
I told my dear lord he's the one I admired
'You did good my son, now you can sing in my choir"

MY LITTLE GIRL JO

As a boy, I grew up in a midwestern town
They said I was the best athlete pound for pound
Sports was always important me
Until one day I blew out my knee
It was many years later my athletics were over
I now had a wife and a dog named Rover
I had a good job, life was sweet
I wanted a son to make life complete
All my friends had sons and they all would boast
A son is what I wanted most
One day my wife said we're having a child
A bundle of joy so tender and mild
When I met my friends at our local diner
I told them all my life couldn't be finer
Like them I hoped to have a son
I'd brag he'd be the toughest son of a gun
That day finally came and to my surprise
We had a beautiful girl with big brown eyes
She wasn't a boy but what a sight to be seen
We decided to name her Josephine
She became a star at both track and at hockey
She was as tender can be, and as tough as Rocky
When she ran track, she was as fast as lightening
She beat all the boys, it was almost frightening
In hockey she would score the winning goal
Against any boy she stood toe to toe
Then came that day I would fear
She said daddy it's time to hang up my gear
She found a young man she truly did love
I prayed for her happiness to heaven above
She got married and sports were now in her past
The next few years flew by real fast
Now my little Jo is having a child
My tough little girl looked so tender and mild
If it's a boy I'm going to name him after you
I said sweetheart I'm praying for a girl just like you

RESILIENT

When you came to Buffalo it was quite a story
With your 'rifle' arm" you brought us to glory
Your resilience rubbed off on our struggling city
Until then all we had was sorrow and pity
A blue-collar town people were leaving
But you came along, and we started believing
The confidence we lacked you had leaps and bounds
Our spirit lifted with your many touchdowns
Our bills started winning, no more crying in our beers
You taught us to face our biggest fears
There was nothing sweeter than Kelly to Reed
You never gave up as our Bills would succeed
It's been many years since us fans saw you throw
And now you are facing a much bigger foe
Jimbo, it's time, put your helmet back on
It's time for us fans to once again bond
Like the warrior you are, get back on the field
You're our knight in armor, with your sword and your shield
Stare down your cancer, it's no match for you
With prayers to our lord, this will get you through
Attack the opponent, show him who's boss
As Marv Levy once said' "there's one more river to cross"
Don't forget who you are, you're Machine Gun Kelly
You have inner strength and grit in your belly
Us fans we will give you our prayers and our love
With your faith you'll get help from the big man above
Like our comeback game there'll be no talk of defeat
With the help of your team this cancer you'll beat
It's our time Jim Kelly, we'll be by your side
There's no place for this cancer to run and hide
Remember this Jimbo, we all got your back
And like Bruce in his day this cancer we'll sack

GOD BLESS AND GOOD LUCK
ONE OF YOUR BIGGEST FANS, LARRY SICURELLA

SET 'EM UP SAM

He quit his job, he's now bartender Sam
A dedicated customer is who I am
I came back to drink and also to vent
To the ladies I meet I'm a respectable gent
Sam's a good listener, he lends us an ear
As people come in and cry in their beer
Politics, sports, world problems we face
To escape for a while there's no better place
We sing karaoke into the wee hours
Sam makes white Russians and the best whiskey sours
Sam never married he is a smart man
Woman really dig him, he has a great tan
Drinks are cheap, his advice we get free
Sam's bar is where me and my friends want to be
This bar is a fraternal organization
I'd rather be here than a family vacation
Sam is real funny, he tells a good joke
I laugh till I cry in my rum and coke
When election time comes we like to debate
We agree things must change before it's too late
The problems are few, I sleep like a log
Two wives have left me, but I still have my dog
Sam has been with me through my divorces
I think Sam could teach psychology courses
I'm not smart or ambitious, I may not go far
But I feel like someone when I walk in this bar

ANGRY OCEAN

The ocean was angry, it had on its mean face
The waves, they were crashing, it not a good place
The seagulls were screeching, they flew out to sea
The temperature's dropping, it's about sixty three
The fog was thick, the water was gray
I thought about leaving but decided to stay
There's a dew in the air but everything's fine
It could have been that bottle of wine
The beach was empty, people fished off the pier
Life is good, there is nothing to fear
Solidarity and peace was what i was after
A good book, some wine and some old fashion laughter
The surfers are surfing, they went out real far
The sun is hidden as I light my cigar
There're joggers, tourists, bikers all around
I love Flagler beach, it's a quaint little town
The town folk, young kids, there's beach bums with abs
The sea shells are plenty there's starfish and crabs
The waves hit the pier where everyone's fishing
Catching the big one is what they are wishing
The clouds are around us way up in the sky
The wind gusts increase, the flags waving high
There's no other place I'd rather be
It's the middle of winter, how lucky are we
There're black birds, white birds, they live on the beach
They fly overhead, they're almost in reach
The jelly fish, the star fish are right off the shore
And the sound that we hear is the mad oceans roar
My mind is clear as I sit on my chair
The sun just came out, I don't have a care
I wish I could stay all day and all night
The ocean and sand makes life feel just right
Thank you, my lord, for all these great treasures
I'm thankful for you and for all life's pleasures

JOE'S BAR

I just had this horrible day at work
I over slept and my boss was a jerk
When I came home and complained to my wife
She looked at me and said get on with your life"
I told her I was going out for some beers
She said have one for me, minus the tears
The walls were closing in, I had to get out
A few beers would be good, I had no doubt
When I got to Joe's bar I was as depressed as could be
As I looked around everyone looked like me
They were crying in their beer, they all looked so sad
How could our lives have gotten so bad?
But this guy had a grin from ear to ear
I noticed there were no tears in his beer
He had it together, I really do think
So, I sat down beside him and bought him a drink
This man just smiled, he said thanks for the beer
But if you came here to cry, please don't sit here
I told him my troubles, he said give me a break
You woke up this morning, for goodness sake
You seem like an intelligent carrying young man
I'm going to tell you a story you might understand
I had my physical just last week
What the doctor told me was bleak
He said I'm a young man of fort two
He said there wasn't much more he could do
I can still hear the doctor telling me
You're not going to make it to forty- three
I cried like a baby as I drove my car
I had no one to talk to, so I went to Joe's bar
Life is fragile, it can be taken away
Enjoy each moment of every day
I never had children or even a wife
I just hoped to make a difference in someone's life
He had a few beers and sat for a while
He said he had made few people smile
You can sit here and drink many more beers

Or go home to your wife but first wipe your tears
His story was touching, he had things figured out
He knew what life was all about
With all his problems and all his strife
He still made a difference in somebody's life
I hugged him and thanked him and wished him good luck
I drank my last beer, then drove off in my truck
When I got home, I hugged my wife
I said I was sorry complaining about life
As we looked at each other nothing had to be said
We cried, then we laughed, then just went to bed

MARV LEVY

One of the greatest coaches I ever knew
He's a scholar, a gentleman, a mentor too
He treated his players like grown men
He motivated them like only Marv can
He had many characters on this great team
Coaching them could be a challenge, or so it would seem
But Marv knew how to handle each one
He coached them like they were his own sons
For Marv they would go through a brick wall
He taught them about team work and how to stand tall
He was all about character he had so much class
He bought pride to our city, not like the past
Our city owes Marv for making us proud
You could see it and feel it when our fans got loud
Those were the days, we loved our bills
It took away stress and all our ills
Marv as a coach couldn't be beat
But being a family man was Marv's greatest feat
You could see the love in Fran levy's eyes
It would melt a heart of any size
She was his beautiful, personable, loving wife
She's his inspiration, the love of his life
They have a daughter that makes their family complete
At home is where Marv don't have to compete
With the like of Kelly, Andre and Bruce
Marv had them ready and rarely would lose
But Marv's legacy will be much more than the game
He will always be in his fan's hall of fame
A Buffalo Bills fan I'll always be
And coach you will always be a hero to me

OLD GLORY

I'll never forget I was a young boy
My grandfather took me to buy a new toy
Grandpa and I were always real close
It was Grandfather's stories that I would love most
Grandpa was smart he had so much knowledge
Though he dropped out of school and never had college
As we walked down this street I saw this old man
He had a hat on his lap and flag in his hand
I turned to grandpa and said who is this guy?
I noticed just then a tear in his eye
He said sit down my son I'll tell you the story
About a proud man they now call old glory
Old glory was a hero a prisoner of war
Now our country turned its back they don't know him no more
A very proud man he saw many friends die
He saw lots of comrades blown out of the sky
This frail old man once handsome and strong
Came back from the war and didn't belong
He has a medal of honor he saved thirty guys
He blew several Japs right out of the sky
He has memories and stories but with no one to share
We turned our back on this hero our country didn't care
When grandpa was done I took my toy back
I put all the money in old glory's hat
I told grandpa I love him and thanks for the story
I had a tear in my eye as I saluted "old glory"

HOSPITALITY

If you sleep over, please make the bed
Help yourself to my food, I want you well fed
You can leave a tip on the kitchen table
And I'll be back as soon as I'm able
Have fun, relax, and think of me
On the beach in Tampa I will be
My home is yours, what could be finer
You can even sit in my favorite recliner

LITTLE ANGELS

As they packed their kid's lunches and sent them to school
It was their last hug but nobody knew
Thinking their children were safe as could be
Brought each parent peace and tranquility
On this fateful day it would change lives forever
The pain and tears would bring parents together
When this coward shot children he might think he had won
But the souls of these angels are stronger than guns
They're now up in heaven, all that's left is the pain
They walk with our Lord, our loss is God's gain
The actions of hero's, ignoring their fears
It's what we'll remember through our grief and our tears
The children are gone, so precious and young
For each of these angels a church bell has rung
Why did this happen, the answers aren't clear
As our "Angels" are in heaven for Christmas this year

NO SWEAT

When I think I can't run one more mile
I run ten more and finish with a smile
At six in the morning when I get up
I head to work with my coffee cup
When I'm done doing pushups and feeling sore
I just suck it up, then do it some more
When I'm doing laps in the swimming pool
The tougher it gets the more laps I do
I wasn't ever an athlete
If you have heart, you can't be beat
It's a little physical and mental too
I ran twenty five marathons and I'm not through
I know what my limitations are
I don't run fast, I do run far
You have to do what you do best
Then do it with vigor and do it with zest
Don't be afraid of a little sweat
It's very fulfilling, the rewards you get
When your body hurts this you'll find
Exercise's good for the body and also the mind

TRANQUILITY

I can feel the tranquility on the oceans beach
Or the stars at night so close I can reach
The beautiful sunset, the bright orange moon
It puts me in a passive mood
The warmth of the sand on a hot summer night
The seashells on the beach are quite a sight
In the early morning I can smell the dew
I love green grass, so moist and cool
Walking in the woods, following the trail
Watching the boats about to sail
If I close my eyes it's very serene
The images are the prettiest I've ever seen
The stillness of the night, the bright sunny day
The long country road, the smell of the hay
The peaceful sound of a running brook
Relaxing at home with an interesting book
As I walk upon some crispy leaves
I know there's a God, I truly believe
How else could you explain all these things?
The fins on a fish, the bird's fragile wings
All this comes from heaven above
From all Gods wisdom and all his love

A LITTLE SOLDIER

One fall day on a September morn
A beautiful boy had just been born
An angel from above, all the love he would give
Who would have thought he would die so we all could live
The little boy looked up at his mom and told her
Someday I'm going to be a soldier
From Boy Scouts to high school it did seem
This cute little boy had but one dream
Some people sit back and ask themselves why
But this young man wasn't afraid to die
He didn't look tough, he had a baby face
At the age of eighteen he was on an army base
His family missed him, they were proud yet torn
They knew he was special the day he was born
It seemed like yesterday he was watching cartoons
Now he was a leader of an army platoon
The letters he sent would fill a sack
His last letter he said he was going to Iraq
What he did next are why heroes are made
With his platoon in danger, he fell on a grenade
With a soldier at their door, they knew what it was about
They have just lost their little boy scout
They'll always have memories of their brave young man
His mom and his dad were his biggest fans

KINDERGARTEN

I was only five and I beg your pardon
It was my very first day in kindergarten
In my sneaker bag I had sneakers and socks
I couldn't wait to play with the building blocks
We were only at school for a half a day
Much to our mothers and fathers dismay
We all took a nap about mid- morning
It made our day a little less boring
Those innocent times, I miss them so
Where did those earlier and simple days go?
Wouldn't it be great to be five forever
At that age we're all cute and clever
I had this crush on Mary Lou
I think she kind of liked me too
We use to study and read together
Her pretty blonde hair was as light as a feather
The thing I liked most was arts and crafts
The things I liked least was science and math
When the day was over and we got on the bus
Sitting by my best friend was a must
When we got home we went out to play
We'd stay outside most of the day
Fifty years later I still can't forget
The prettiest girl I ever met
Mary Lou and I became husband and wife
From kindergarten to now I had a great life

MIND READER

Imagine reading a person's mind
The deep dark secrets you would find
You could figure out what makes them tick
Why certain people do not click
You'd know when someone was truthful or lying
You'd know the reason they were crying
The mind is a dangerous thing I know
Pressures and stress can take a toll
It could be scary to know how they feel
Are they ingenious, are they for real
Imagine a politician's mind
If you looked inside is it corruption you'd find
Sometimes it's better not to know
Do you want to go deep into someone's soul?
Would it be better to trust a person instead?
Should you believe their words being said?
The mystery of life would sure be gone
To know what they're thinking simply seems wrong
Would you want someone reading your mind?
Could you imagine the things they would find?
What's in somebody's mind is just a small part
What's important is the love that's in their heart
I guess what I'm really trying to say
If we trust our hearts we'll all be okay

NEW YEAR RESOLUTIONS

When taking a bus I'll give up a seat
I'll help an old lady crossing the street
That homeless person I'll give him some change
I'll listen to their story no matter how strange
I'll make some soup and share it with friends
I'll stay calm no matter how the game ends
I'll learn a new word every day
Take my parents to dinner and not let them pay
I'll visit an old person in a nursing home
Each day I'll write an inspiring poem
I'll tell my family I love them so
I'll say hi to strangers everywhere I go
I'll put away some money for a rainy day
I'll help a lost person find their way
I'll pray for the sick, and not miss mass
I'll call a dear friend from the past
I'll get a physical and exercise too
I'll buy my dog a bone to chew
I'll pray for our soldiers and last but not least
I'll help clothe the poor and cook them a feast

FOOD FOR THOUGHT

I love food, the more the better
I follow each recipe to the letter
Soups and salads I love to devour
And I love to eat at any hour
I like to eat healthy to live a long life
I want to grow old with my children and wife
Once in a while I eat a snack
Though I know it's nutrients that they lack
Veggies and fruits are where it's at
I try to stay away from saturated fat
Steaks and hamburgers really taste great
But eating red meats, you're testing your fate
Turkey and chicken are better for you
They're good for your heart and cholesterol too
I love apples, bananas, carrots and peas
I also love honey from the honey bees
I ate healthy foods over the years
I also ate onions but they brought me to tears
I now see the rewards of eating right
As I get older I see the light
So instead of eating a bag of chips
Only healthy food will pass these lips

MYRTLE BEACH

The soft white sand of Myrtle Beach
The stars at night you can almost reach
The wind blowing softly upon your face
Myrtle Beach is a very special place
As I gaze at the ocean down below
I sit on my balcony and forget my woe
The sound off the waves as I close my eyes
The sun each morning, we watch it rise
You can sit by the pool or take a swim
You can go to the ocean on a whim
You can walk on the beach in the early morn
When you finish your walk you'll feel reborn
Tourists are fishing off the pier
If you listen at night it's foghorns you'll hear
There's a little clam stand down the road
It smells real good if truth be told
If it's serenity that you wish to find
Sit by the ocean with a bottle of wine
As you walk the beach late at night
The moon shining down is a glorious sight
The people are great, a little laid back
They move slower here, that's a matter of fact
The seafood's definitely the best around
There are seafood restaurants all through the town
If you're looking for heaven it's the closest you'll find
It's great for your soul and cleanses your mind

RABBIT EARS

What I recall most of my childhood years
Was our old TV with rabbit ears?
Life was much simpler way back then
There was no E-mail, just paper and pen
Saturday nights I'll never forget
My dad watched westerns on our old TV set
Television shows were done in good taste
Our lives were moving at a much slower pace
Our television set had poor reception
But we didn't notice, it was all about perception
The whole family watched TV together
We kids went outside when we had good weather
We weren't couch potatoes, we stayed pretty fit
All we needed was a ball and a baseball mitt
There weren't computers or internet
The books I read I'll never forget
I sometimes wish I was still there
The long country roads and the smell of fresh air
We went horseback riding at my uncle's farm
A day in the country worked like a charm
We were city folk but that was okay
We all felt like farmers, if for only a day
We fed the chickens and horses too
Milking the cows, I thought was cool
On Sundays our family all went to church
And the only soda we drank was root beer or birch
You can keep your computers and cable TV
Our old "Rabbit Ears" worked perfect for me

BUFFALO MARATHON

The Buffalo marathon is quite unique
If it's beauty and scenery that you seek
The course is flat, you could have a fast time
There are very few hills that you must climb
The field is small so you can get a good start
Forest Lawn cemetery is my favorite part
The Erie Marina is quite a sight
The breeze off the lake hits you just right
The ethnic neighborhoods are really a treat
It helps you forget your aching feet
Delaware Park is at twenty one miles
When you reach that point you notice the smiles
They have volunteers who serve Gatorade
It's about that time your body starts to fade
I need more water but I had my fill
The journey to the finish is mostly downhill
The weather in May is really nice
But you train all winter, you do pay a price
It's almost over, you can see downtown
The stomping of feet is the only sound
When you hit City Hall the finish is near
All you can think of is that nice cold beer
It's important to finish wearing a smile
Because you just ran twenty six miles
It was all worth it, the cold months you train
It was zero degrees, you must be insane
I live in Buffalo and I might be a fool
But this keeps me in shape at age fifty two

MY LEGACY

How will my loved ones remember me?
I pray it's the good things that they see
I'd try much harder to do some good
I'd change some things if I could
If truth be told, I can't complain
I had lots of sunshine, with not much rain
The words I spoke came from my heart
I tried to fit in and do my part
There were times in my life I had no answer
I tried to help children afflicted with cancer
I tried to put laughter back in their life
I felt their pain and it cut like a knife
I hope I'm remembered for my big smile
Or running marathons, mile after mile
I hope my poems made someone happy
At times they're long and a little bit sappy
I hope I'm remembered for giving my all
Or the good in people that I saw
I loved playing drums, we had a good band
My mother and father were my biggest fans
I loved my family and I loved my dog
With unconditional love, you can't go wrong
The very last thing I'd like to say
Enjoy each precious second of each precious day

RUSH HOUR

I get to bed late, I set the alarm
I get up at eight, so what's the harm
I eat a fast breakfast then hurry to dress
As I run out the door I'm really a mess
I have twenty five minutes to get to work
I can't be late, my boss is a jerk
When I arrive at work I'm all wound up
As I pour some coffee in my cup
I made work on time so there is no worry
But it seems every day, I'm more in a hurry
When I get home, there's work to be done
Doing yard work is not really fun
I try to finish before the sun goes down
That's all I do is rush around
I work all day then work all night
Life must slow down, this just isn't right
We rush to go here, we rush to go there
But are we really going somewhere
As we hurry through life it passes us by
And as we get older time seems to fly
Weeks turn to months, months turn to years
It's enough to bring an old man to tears
With computers and cell phones it's hard to slow down
Life's got so loud, I can't hear a sound
Take one morning and go for a walk
Listen to nature, there's no need to talk
Find a calm place, then read a good book
Or maybe go fishing, put a worm on a hook
Our seconds and minutes are ticking away
Our journey in life will end someday
So take a deep breath, do what you love
And pray to sweet Jesus in heaven above

MY LIBRARY

It's just a building, but at a closer look
It's what's inside that could fill a book
As you browse the shelves there's so much to see
There's no better place than the library
There are movies, music and computers too
That's why the library is so very cool
It's a place you can travel to the moon
Travel the world all before noon
You can see the Nile River, or New York City
You could read a good novel or just something witty
If your kids are bored or feeling blue
In the children's section there's plenty to do
There are journals, maps and books of mystery
If you are nostalgic there's lots of history
The librarians will help you find your way
You'll never have a more memorable day
When you are done and checking out
You'll want to come back, I have no doubt
You've been here all day and learned a ton
Your children read books and had lots of fun

REMEMBER

It's finally here, Memorial Day
The first day of summer, some people would say
Hotdogs, cookouts, family and friends
It's an all day picnic that never ends
The beer is flowing, it's eighty degrees
The flowers are blooming, there are honey bees
As I start to grill, I begin to reflect
About all our veterans, we must not forget
World War one and World War two
Korea, Vietnam and the Iraq war too
It's our sons, brothers and fathers who fought
It's a lesson in bravery that can't be taught
The women who fought, we salute you
You were so brave, you're the red, white and blue
As we put a burger on a roll
A soldier is fighting from his fox hole
As I cookout all day with my sons and my wife
These soldiers are fighting for our great life
When we see the fireworks and hear the band
Think of our soldiers fighting in the hot sand
They sacrifice for you and also for me
So we can have peace and we can be free
When we complain about high prices we must pay
Our soldiers just want to see the next day
These soldiers are young, some only eighteen
Yet the horrors of war they have already seen
They are there to defend the red, white and blue
They are trained to be the best at what they do
So when you go to bed please say a prayer
For all our "BRAVE SOLDIERS" fighting somewhere

FLORIDA'S CALLING

From the tip of Miami to St. Augustine
It's the closest to heaven I've ever seen
The orange Florida moon the St. Augustine sun
The fountain of youth where I hope to get young
It's been a tough year, but somehow I got through
I'm on a journey to Florida, soon my dreams will come true
St. Augustine has some beautiful parks
And Daytona lights up each night after dark
I'll drive my Marquee down to Palm Coast
I'll stop for some shrimp, that's what I love most
I've lived here in Buffalo, I've dealt with the snow
I've been thinking about Florida for ten years or so
No more cold winters, I'm now Florida bound
Its peace of mind I have found
The blue coral ocean, the crystal white sand
There's no prettier scenery in our great land
So as I start my new life, and my journey ends
Here's a message I'd like to send
I'm now in Florida and here I will stay
If there's one thing I know, life gets better each day

MY DREAM JOB

If I had one wish I'd be boss for a day
Then I would have the final say
Besides all the money I would make
I could take a long lunch and a half hour break
I'd have an office with a view of the city
I'd be real smart and very witty
I'd have a big desk and a comfortable chair
I'd give no explanations, I don't have to be fair
I could arrive at work at any time
I'd have my own elevator, no stairs to climb
My workers would like me or they'd be fired
With no physical work, I'd never get tired
You could bribe this boss to get ahead
You need this job so your family is fed
My opinion is the only one that would count
I should never be questioned as problems mount
On second thought there's not enough pay
To be the boss for even one day
Being a father and husband is what I want to be
There's nothing as important as my family

FUTURE IS NOW

My future is now, not tomorrow
I've experienced bliss and also sorrow
I must stay focused and live for today
I really can't worry what people say
I'm wild and carefree, I am a good man
I help my neighbors whenever I can
Sometimes I wish my life would slow down
I like sitting in the woods, hearing nature's sounds
I owe nothing to no one, I can look in the mirror
The future looks great, there's nothing I fear
I cry during movies, and I really hate war
I pray for violence to be no more
I have no agenda, I do my own thing
I have no great voice but I love to sing
I go to church whenever I can
I am very respectful, I don't mean to offend
Don't tell me it's raining if it's not
Don't tell me it's cold when it really is hot
I have a soft spot for kids that are ill
I have to stay busy, I can't stand still
I stay away from trouble whenever I can
Here's the main message I like to send
"We're only here for a little while
So stay true to yourself and continue to smile

CROSSROADS OF LIFE

What in God's name are we going to do?
There's too much violence and we don't have a clue
Does violence breed violence, I really hope not
With all this fighting, is it peace we forgot?
It doesn't make any sense, all this killing
In our once peaceful streets there's lots of blood spilling
Innocent children being taken from us
As our nation hates and protesters cuss
They are our children and we must show them the way
If we don't straighten this out, there's a price we will pay
If our children get bored, they must find a hobby
No more guns in the streets, this we must lobby
Nobody's perfect, you can all still have some fun
But don't cross that line, don't hurt anyone
Life is so fragile, we can't take it for granted
We must live in peace, we have but one planet
We can't do it alone, we can't wait anymore
No more fighting, no more war
We're in this together, and at the very least
We must teach our kids to grow up in peace
Imagining not locking your doors at night
Or caring if someone's skin is black or white
We're all at the crossroads and we can't look back
There's no more talking, it's time to act
With a lots of work and a little praying
We must give peace a chance, that's all I am saying

MEANING OF CHRISTMAS

Christmas is coming, it's that time of year
But its meaning sometimes isn't quite clear
It's about baby Jesus or did we forget
It's not about presents that we all get
It's not about fighting for that last toy
Christmas is supposed to be filled with joy
It's about good tidings, family and friends
And the meaning of Christmas the season sends
Think about giving a present to a stranger
Or taking the family to see a live manger
Giving gifts this year, I think I will pass
I'll feed the homeless then go to Mass
I won't worry about buying the new play station
These games are destroying our younger generation
The worth of your gift is not what you spend
It's the happiness and love that you spread
Christmas don't have to be such a peril
It's all about singing a Christmas carol
So this year I'm sending prayers as a gift
It's a gift that will give you a spiritual lift
As we celebrate Christmas it will become clear
The gift of prayer will be with you all year

A PERFECT DAY

I woke up this morning and rubbed my eyes
Early to bed, early to rise
I felt the calmness in the air
I felt pain free and for me that is rare
The weekend was here, I had yard work to do
I'll do it all early while the weather is cool
The dew was thick, the wind was brisk
What a beautiful morning, the air was crisp
It was a great day to take a long run
As soon as all my chores were done
When I finished my run I took a long shower
I then take a nap for about a half hour
It was way too nice to stay inside
So I hopped in my truck and took a long ride
The day was young, the sun was bright
The sky was blue, what a beautiful sight
As I drove in the country my mind did wander
I thought about life and I started to ponder
How lucky I was to be this healthy
I have a great family and that makes me wealthy
I realize I'm blessed in so many ways
And I know this was a perfect day

A CHILD'S FACE

Did you ever study the face of a child?
It's very innocent, it's tender and mild
I love seeing children at Christmas time
It makes you forget all the hate and crime
Have you seen a child on Santa's lap?
Or their angelic faces as they take a nap
These beautiful children are yours and mine
It's through their love, the happiness we find
The funny expressions and their silly faces
Makes you forget their untied laces
A bad day at work will go away
One hug from a child makes things okay
At night while watching the evening news
It's very depressing, it gives you the blues
You see little children dying from cancer
I hope someday they find an answer
I turn the channel to another station
I see young kids fighting in other nations
With guns in their hands it makes me cry
I put my head in my hands and ask myself why
So as I pray for the children in heaven above
May we find peace and tranquility through a child's love

MY THOUGHTS

Look over your shoulder, what do you see
I see an angel helping me
How do you act when you have strife?
I look for ways to improve my life
What do you do when you are depressed?
I give to others and do with less
When tragedy hits what do you do
I try to move on, I hope to get through
When life gets confusing and i don't have a clue
I search for answers and you can too
When it rains or snows do you just lay around
It's a good time get up, go out on the town
What do you do when you can't sleep?
Do you drink warm milk, then count sheep
When I'm running late and the boss seems mad
I think of the good days that I had
These are my thoughts, some good some bad
Most are happy, very few sad

JUST SMILE

Are daily problems getting you down?
Do you walk around wearing a frown?
Do you feel some days you're going insane?
Do people say you always complain?
As I jog each day mile after mile
One thing's for sure, I'm wearing a smile
People ask if my life is good
I tell them someday I think it could
Why worry about things I can't control
Life's too short, just let it go
When I cross the marathon finish line
A smile on my face is what you'll find
I'm hurting and aching more than you know
But I'm really proud and I let it show
American soldiers are fighting and dying
But I've never seen a soldier crying
Self-pity will never be a part of me
A glass half full is all I can see
I bring laughter and smiles to work each day
Laughter's contagious, that's what they say
If I could just make one person smile
They'd forget their problems for a little while
The years fly by way too fast
It's your memories and good times that really last
It's not how much money in your bank account
What you give to others is what life's all about
So the next time you're walking down the street
Smile at strangers that you meet
Give thanks each day when you awake
And feel blessed for each friend that you make

BLESS OUR HOUSE

Bless our house, our sweet Lord
It's a modest house that we can afford
Please bless our belongings, though we do have few
Bless our food and our kitchen too
Please shelter us from the long winter cold
Bless our furnace, it is very old
Keep happiness in and sorrow out
Love is what our home is about
Could you please put out the welcome mat?
Home is where you hang your hat
Keep the positive in, the negative out
Bring us your smiles, there's no time to pout
Could you bless our basement which I truly love?
Could you watch our house from heaven above?
Could you keep us all safe in our swimming pool?
Could you bless our front yard and back yard too?
Could you bless our guests and get them home safe
Before every meal we will show you our faith
We pray in our house no fights will be heard
We will pray against evil and follow your word

FIREMEN (OUR HEROS)

It's three in the morning there's two feet of snow
The fire alarm rings and you have to go
You run out the door and don't make a peep
The rest of your family is fast asleep
When you reach the station you jump on the truck
You want God on your side and a little luck
With sirens blazing on this cold dreary night
Your destination is now insight
You hook up the hoses then go inside
In the dark flaming house you pray nobody died
You hear children screaming, you try to fight through
This is what you are trained to do
You don't get paid extra, you're just doing your job
There are times you come home and break down and sob
You put out a fire or save someone's life
You come home and hug your children and wife
Sometimes it gets a little tough
You think that maybe you had enough
You share your stories over a couple of beers
There's plenty of laughter and a couple tears
What gets you through the lows and highs?
Is the pride and love in your family's eyes?
So next time you leave your children and spouse
Take the Lord along into that burning house

MARATHON OF LIFE

As I wait for the marathon in another two days
I ponder how a marathon is like life in some ways
It's not how you start, it's how you end
You run up the hills and around the bends
It's a journey I started as a humble young boy
It's a tedious road so relax and enjoy
It's not what happens but how you react
It tests your endurance, that's a fact
You must have stamina if you want to endure
If you run a smart race, you'll finish for sure
You might not be gifted but your heart they can't gage
You accomplish your goals at any age
Along the way sometimes you'll be sad
You'll feel more pain than you ever had
Pain is temporary, your rewards are not
When you cross the finish line it will mean a lot
Except the challenges that you will meet
I complained about blisters then I saw a man without feet
Be true to yourself, show people you care
It's not just the journey, it's how you got there

MAJESTIC LETCHWORTH PARK

The leaves are majestic the colors are bright
Letchworth in autumn is a beautiful sight
The gorge is so deep, the river runs wild
In early October the weather is mild
The deer are running, so graceful and sleek
Woodpeckers chop away with their sharp beaks
The season is changing, you feel it in the air
It won't be long until the trees are bare
There are long winding roads throughout Letchworth Park
It's a beautiful sunset as it starts to get dark
You can see the trestle that the trains often cross
The dew on the grass from the early morning frost
The skunks can be spotted in the early fall
If they happen to spray it's smelled by us all
Campfires burn throughout this great park
You can smell the aroma from the burning bark
As I hike down this long and winding path
I see swans in the lake taking a bath
There's no better place I'd rather be
I feel like the wildlife, totally free
Down by the Iris we watch the hawks fly
They're a sight to behold up in the sky
From the colorful leaves to the birds up above
It's Letchworth Park that I love

RETIREMENT

I can't believe I'm retiring soon
The first day I think I'll sleep to noon
Thirty one years, most of them good
I worked real hard but had fun when I could
The friends I made I'll have for life
Now I can spend more time with my wife
I'll clean my clubs, they look pretty dusty
I'll paint my bike, it's a little rusty
I'll sit on the porch, smell the dew in the morning
Watching the sunrise will never get boring
Waving to my friends as they go to work
Smell the fresh coffee as it starts to perk
I'm only fifty five and life is real great
I'll never again worry about getting up late
It's a reality now, no more wishing
My priority now are golfing and fishing
At a cancer camp I'll volunteer
My job is to bring happiness and spread some cheer
I can go to Tampa, Orlando too
I can work at Disney by Winnie the Pooh
I have lots of plans but I'm in no hurry
Life is fun now, no need to worry
If you call me in March and I'm hard to reach
I might be at Miami Beach

GRAY SKIES

Wide right, no goal
Cheating politicians, our share of snow
Six months of winter, high energy bills
It's enough to test the toughest of wills
Losing seasons year after year
There's not a big enough glass to cry in my beer
Slushy streets cloudy skies
When our kids finish college they say their goodbyes
We have no projects, just study after study
You're only employed if you're a politician's buddy
We're going to pot, just take a good look
All this corruption, I could write a book
The Indians are trying to build a casino
But with our backward mayor, we'll never be Reno
Our streets are decaying, it's really a shame
And nobody wants to take the blame
They raise our taxes, they claim there's no money
It's really a joke, but it isn't too funny
When are we going to get a break?
Will we ever build something on our great lake?
Let's win the Cup or Super Bowl
So our city could finally get on a roll

HEADLESS BIKER

As I jogged in the Cemetery late last night
Out of the darkness came this strange sight
There was this man on a bike coming at me
But his head on his shoulder I could not see
He hit me then rode down this long dark road
All I had was a scrape when all was told
What I saw next scared me out of my wits
Next to this grave was where his head sits
This headless biker ran over me
And his head at the grave was all I could see
What did I do to deserve this fate?
How did he get through the cemetery gate?
The very next night I went back for a run
I wasn't going to let a ghost ruin my fun
Should I start running during the day?
Would my night time running end this way
When I glanced at the gravestone where the head was laying
I saw this old man and I heard him praying
He said, "I once was a man who had a dream
Until this trucker ran over me
I was a great biker but this I did learn
You can't outrace a trucker coming around the turn"

WARM HANDS

Your hands are warm, while your heart is cold
I don't know if I can go down this road
There's so many roadblocks and detours ahead
I don't know if I can do this again
You say you love me, I've heard that before
The first year's a blast, the second's a war
You said you were different from all the rest
I heard that before, I must confess
You're a beautiful girl, inside and out
It's not the inside I'm worried about
When you walk in a bar, heads are turning
My heart is pounding, my stomach's churning
I'm getting to old, I don't want to fight
I just want to relax on a Saturday night
It's nothing you do or nothing you say
I don't know why I'm feeling this way
I guess I've been hurt over the years
There's been to many shots and to many tears
I wish I could trust in a woman again
I do want a lover, who could be my best friend
You told me once you gave me your heart
And I know how I feel when we are apart
So put on your boots and pretty red dress
Let's do the town, that's what we do best
You'll attract all the guys but that's alright
Because you're going home with this cowboy tonight

AMERICAN DREAM

I can still smell grandma's sweet apple pie
And seeing the bluebirds up in the sky
Families all worshiped on Sunday morning
Our lives were much simpler, though never boring
Dad worked two jobs while mom stayed home
And our little picket fence was as far as we'd roam
I remember the Beatle's on the Ed Sullivan show
The Viet Nam war was taking a toll
I remember the day John F. Kennedy was shot
And I remember the flower children smoking pot
The space age was here, we put a man on the moon
I remember at Woodstock, A Janice Joplin tune
Each summer on weekends we'd head to the beach
Our parents made sure our goals we would reach
Our family values meant something then
Our young hearts broke, but somehow they would mend
We had sport stars like Namath and Willie Mays
There was Bobby Hull and speedy Bob Hayes
The peace movement started, there was discrimination
Equality and peace was our destination
Our parents worried when we changed our ways
Beatle haircuts and boots were the new craze
We were a little rebellious, we thought we were cool
History was being written but who had a clue
High School dances were really great
On Saturday mornings was our high school debate
Like all good things, they must come to an end
But this message to our children we must send
Through the good times and bad, as our love ones depart
Enjoy your youth and follow your heart

MY COUNTRY GIRL

My heart is throbbing, my head's in a swirl
As I listen to my favorite country girl
She belts out ballads, she makes men cry
She sings about husbands who cheat and lie
She has golden blonde hair that gets tossed in the wind
She sings about places she's already been
I never get tired of seeing her show
I always get tickets in the very first row
She once tipped her hat directly at me
That is pure country hospitality
She sings about cheating and sadness to us
Then it's back on the road in her touring bus
I love seeing her in her tight blue jeans
But it's not just her looks by any means
She gives me goosebumps when she sings a sad song
She sings about places I feel I belong
For such a young girl she knows about life
As she sings about a man's cheating wife
I'm amazed how much talent one girl could possess
And the next song she sings is always her best
I'm not a cowboy but I know for sure
If I had a cold, she'd be the cure

TEARS ON MY PILLOW

I crawl out of bed, its frigid cold
My bones are creaking, I feel so old
Outside I see our weeping willow
I lay inside with tears on my pillow
My mother is dying, she doesn't have long
My heart is breaking, something feels wrong
How could my mother be so tough?
Some days I feel I had enough
My dad is a rock, he is so brave
He's resilient and strong like a tidal wave
I try to stay strong and pray to our Lord
That he someday slays cancer with his mighty sword
Every day I wake I wipe my tears
I can't stop thinking of happier years
My mom is sweet, yet very strong
She always could fix whatever went wrong
My dad was a hard worker in every sense
We had a cute little house with a white picket fence
As my mom lays in bed I can't help but think
Life goes by fast, as quick as a blink
I know life goes on, yet I do miss those days
When life was much simpler in many ways
We've been blessed as a family for so many years
We shared lots of laughter and a couple of tears
I won't say goodbye, we'll be together someday
And there'll be no more tears to wipe away

BOY SOLDIER

It's been twelve long months here in Iraq
I miss my family, I can't wait to get back
Each day I'm here it's getting tougher
I'll never get used to seeing kids suffer
One day I get a letter from my wife
She loves someone else, she wants a new life
My heart is breaking, tears streaming down
I can't even think as I walk through this town
My life is crumbling but what can I do
I have a war to fight, I must try to get through
Wounded soldiers are everywhere
I'm fighting for her, doesn't she care
My best friend here lost his life today
He loved his country, the ultimate price he did pay
My mouth is so dry from all his sand
I can't even eat, this food is so bland
When I was young I thought soldiers were cool
I thought someday that's what I would do
I had visions of being a war time hero
Well I got my wish when they hit ground zero
This is what I was trained to do
My platoon got ready and off we flew
I would never admit I was afraid
My allegiance to my country has never swayed
I'm proud to wear my army tags
But I'm sick of seeing body bags
I write my wife and this I told her
"You broke my heart but I'm a soldier
I'm happy for you, I've cried my last tear
I have to focus on the war over here
My spirit was shaken, but I will mend
To everyone home my love I send"

NO MORE VIOLENCE

Look around, what do you see?
People are dying needlessly
Guns and knives are there for the taking
Our nation is in for a rude awakening
Kids in the streets, where's mom and dad
These punks are scary, that makes us all mad
Violence isn't the answer, it's just an excuse
You forgot your meds, you're shot up with juice
It's time to say no, we won't take it no more
We must stop violence like never before
If you pull the trigger and hurt someone
It's you I blame, not the gun
Violence breeds violence, it's really a pity
It's everywhere, not just in the city
I won't give forgiveness or accept remorse
Let the criminal system take its course
We worry about the gunman, we see his mom cry
The victim's family just wants to know why
You've destroyed people's lives because you felt like it
I don't feel sorry for you, not one bit
You're still alive, you're still walking
The person you shot isn't even talking
Your upbringing will only get you so far
You are responsible for who you are
When you use a weapon at any age
You should be put away, we don't want your rage
When you hurt someone, you better think first
As things for you could get a lot worse

CAMP CLOSED

It was early July, a hot humid day
The bus arrived, we'd be soon on our way
The older campers are excited, some younger campers cry
The kids hugged their parents, they said their goodbyes
These kids all have cancer but you'd never know
I wish I had an ounce of the courage they show
It takes us three hours, the bus ride is long
We try to pass time with stories and song
We finally arrive but somethings not right
There's no one to greet us, there's no one in sight
The infirmary is closed, no nurse to be found
The camp looks deserted, there isn't a sound
What could have happened, how could this be
The cabins are locked, and no one has keys
There's no woodshop or music, there's no arts and crafts
There's no children with counselors, there's no hearty laughs
There's no lifeguard on duty, no boats on the shore
No skits by the camp fire, no kids eating Smores
Where would these kids go to forget all their pain?
To conquer they're fears, play ball in the rain
I then noticed this sign as we pulled away
In big bold letters this is what it did say

THANK YOU, CAMPERS AND COUNSELORS,
FOR ALL THE GREAT YEARS
THE SMILES, THE LAUGHTER AND ALSO THE TEARS
EVERY SICK CHILD WHO WALKED DOWN TEDDI LANE
WE HOPE THAT WE HELPED EASE SOME OF YOUR PAIN
I PRAYED EVERY NIGHT FOR THESE CHILDREN SO PURE
THEY'D NO LONGER HAVE CANCER
BECAUSE THEY FOUND A CURE
WELL I'M HAPPY TO SAY 'THERE IS NO MORE CANCER
THE DOCTORS GOT TOGETHER, AND THEY FOUND THE ANSWER
I THANK THE DEAR LORD FOR HIS GUIDANCE AND LOVE
FOR TAKING CARE OF OUR CHILDREN IN HEAVEN ABOVE

"CAMP GOODAYS IS CLOSED" IT SAID ON THE SIGN
NO MORE SICK CHILDREN, IT'S ABOUT TIME"

DOG DAYS OF WINTER

My car doors are frozen, it's zero degrees
I put on my thermos so I don't freeze
I haven't seen a plow for a couple of hours
I can't remember when I last saw flowers
My car doors now open but my car won't start
So I shovel the driveway which is bad for the heart
My neighbors look cranky as I drive down the street
Everything's frozen, even my feet
The car's really cold, the heater's not working
I should have stayed home where the coffee was perking
The streets are pure ice, visibility is poor
It's a cold winter morning that is for sure
When I get to work I'm a Popsicle stick
I'm cold, I' m wet, I bet I get sick
When I try to dry off I begin to sneeze
Someone hand me a tissue please
I need some coffee, I am so cold
The coffee looks about ten days old
I hear the boss yelling, he really looks mad
Thank goodness it's Friday, what a week I had
It's not even pay week, I'm as broke as could be
My money goes fast, there's nothing for free
The sun just came out for a minute or two
Why can't the sky be sunny and blue?
This is our winter in our great city
I wish it was summer, it is a real pity
As I sit in my house, it's cold and damp
The only light I see is the living room lamp
Two more years before I retire
I'll go to Disney and hope to get hired
I live for today, but can't wait for tomorrow
I'll write poems by the ocean and forget all my sorrow

FORGOTTEN DREAMS

The older I get the more it seems
I have a lot of forgotten dreams
Our memory fades or so they say
I wish I could remember yesterday
When my first girlfriend left, who was the blame?
I can't even remember her first name
My memories have faded but I had a blast
Though I don't remember much from my past
As I get older my future looks bright
I can still see the beauty, because I still have my sight
Memory loss is not that bad
Because I forget, I barely stay mad
You can call me a bum or say I am rotten
And the very next day all is forgotten
If you owe me some money do not fret
Chances are good that I will forget
I had this nice car and did I ever boast
I lost it one day on the west coast
My wife just left me because she got sore
When I couldn't remember where I lived any more
Life's too short and my memory is too
Now what was I saying, I don't have a clue
I have some money that I hid somewhere
I forgot where it is, but I don't really care
I took medication about an hour ago
What I took it for, I don't really know
I like to watch football for the glory and fame
But when it's all over I forget who won the game
I can watch the same movie or read a book twice
If I could remember, I'd take your advice
Having said all of this one thing I would bet
There are things in my life I'd rather forget

A HOT TAMALE AND A SHOT OF TEQUILA

It's time to leave old Buffalo
I'm heading down to New Mexico
Where those "hot" tamales are looking fine
I can picture those beauties in my mind
My wife just left me and I need some tequila
It won't take long to find me a diva
She'll be pretty and young and totally tan
We'll drink all day then lay in the sand
She'll help me forget my cheating wife
And help me forget my miserable life
I'd much rather party then shovel snow
I should have done this years ago
I'll wear my sombrero and Mexican beads
There's not much more that I would need
A few tequilas and a Mexican tune
Sitting under a Mexican moon
What better place could I be?
To feel alive and totally free
I won't drink the water, but I'll eat their great food
By now I'll be in a tranquil mood
Mexico is one big fiesta
I'll party to dawn then take a siesta
They say I am living in paradise
It's never boring, time really flies
Those dreary days in Buffalo
Are barely a memory in Mexico?
No more hustle, no more work
Sleeping to noon, it is a great perk
I'm only a tourist but I feel right at home
It's now in Mexico where I roam

THE OLD MAN ON THE BENCH

One day I was walking in the park
I saw this old man in the dark
His clothes were messy, his hair was wind blown
He looked so sad, he was all alone
I said to this man I don't mean to pry
You look so sad, may I ask why
This little old man in his old black coat
Could barely talk and cried when he spoke
He said how he wanted to live a long life
But that all changed when he lost his wife
As this little old man continued to talk
I totally forgot about my walk
I could feel his sadness and could see his tears
He said growing old was his number one fear
He said he had lost his first true love
And he prays every night to Jesus above
He tells his sweet Lord if he could be so bold
He's ready to die, he don't want to grow old
His children are gone and so is his wife
There's not much left in this man's life
With that being said he got up and went
I tried to figure out what all this meant
I have to admit I really felt bad
I wished him the best but I could tell he was sad
The next time I took a walk in the park
There was a tree near that bench and writing on the bark
In big bold letters this is what it said:
"If I'm not here I'm probably dead
I'm now with my sweetheart in heaven above
And with my dear children who I truly love

TRUE CHAMPION

I'm at Madison Square Garden, the Anthem just sung
The fighters are ready, the bell has just rung
I love a good fight but here is the thing
I love my son more and he's in the ring
The championship of the world is what's at stake
I really am nervous, I can feel myself shake
My son looks at me and gives me a wink
My mind is muddled, I can't hardly think
My son threw an uppercut to his chin
He had to hit and move if he wanted to win
The fight got intense in the second round
My son took a punch and almost went down
He looked at me, he was all right
He got stronger and faster, he got into the fight
As round six started he had blood in his eye
I am a grown man yet I started to cry
That's my boy out there, he is all I got
My stomach was all tied in a knot
Round eight just started, I am glued to my seat
Both fighters were bloody, they both looked beat
They both hung on, the punches were few
Just then my son said, "Dad, this one's for you"
He delivered a punch right to his head
This fighter went down like a ton of lead
The ref started counting, it seemed real slow
Both fighters were great, they put on a good show
Then as my head started to swirl
They announced my son was "Champion of the world"
When he winked at me my eyes filled with tears
I'll remember that moment for the rest of my years

DENTIST APPOINTMENT

You should go to the dentist at any cost
Brushing's important but you also must floss
Take care of your teeth, don't wait till you're old
Your teeth are worth more than silver or gold
If you don't have cavities you're a lucky fellow
If you don't get a cleaning your teeth will turn yellow
Next time you go let me give you this tip
Keep still or the dentist will drill your lip
Don't eat too much candy or too much cake
The next thing you know you have a toothache
If you're visiting the dentist for a filling
"Be brave young man", don't fear the drilling
If you didn't have a cleaning for quite a while
Make an appointment today and continue to smile

GODS CREATIONS

Did you ever just listen to the wind?
The swirling and whistling around the bend
Have you heard the crickets on a quiet night?
Or see the sun rising, what a beautiful sight
Did you ever see a star constellation?
How can we think we're not Gods Creation?
The beautiful colors of leaves each fall
Or the sound in the forest, the owls call
Have you ever seen the river flow?
Or the different shape flakes in the winter snow
Did you ever get up early and smell the dew
Or wonder why the sky is so blue
Did you ever wonder who created trees?
Or taste the honey from the honey bees
The eagle flying gracefully way up above
The natural beauty of a morning dove
Have you witnessed the calmness of the lake?
This is God's work, it's no mistake
So some day when you are totally bored
Take a walk outside and see the work of our Lord

WINTER

AS I glance outside it looks so cold
The snow's piled up along the road
It's a winter wonderland, a storybook scene
Winter's begun, the snow looks so clean
The birds all flew south a month ago
They normally leave before the first snow
So I bundle up and venture outside
I get on board for a long winter ride
It's not a surprise, it comes every year
But we're never quite sure when the first flake will appear

LONG COLD WINTER

It's another cold winter in our fair city
I wish it was summer, oh what a pity
The snow's coming down, the streets are a mess
I wish I was in Florida away from this stress
In our city it snows six months a year
Someday it may snow nine months I fear
We only get sunshine for a couple of hours
It will be a long time before we see flowers
People are miserable, you can't blame them much
The winter really packs quite a punch
We can only dream of the coming summer
It's winter now, it's really a bummer
The snow, the ice, the hail and the sleet
The frozen fingers and frozen feet
We have six months of hibernation
When we finally see light, it's a celebration
So each night I stay in and play solitary
Going out in this weather can really be scary
As I look out the window it's a winter wonderland
I dream of the beaches and the hot white sand

MY FRIENDS, MY RICHES

I could have money, silver and gold
But its friends I want most when I grow old
Wealth would not be all that bad
But without my friends I'd be lonely and sad
To have someone there to say good morning
Friends make life a little less boring
To have someone there to lend a hand
To lend an ear whenever they can
I know wealthy people and that's all right
But money won't comfort or say good night
If you have one good friend that's a lot
I thank the Lord each night for the friends I got
My friends are all special, they're very unique
The love in their hearts is what I seek
What I'm trying to say is if my ship don't come in
With all my friends a great life it has been

ALL GODS CREATION

AS the bluebird sings each early morn
The robins in the nest were recently born
The smell of the grass and the cool fresh air
You could see the Lords work everywhere
You know there's a God, just look around
Walk in a woods and hear nature's sounds
See the honey bees around their hive
It makes you appreciate being alive
Lookup to the sky, way up above
Then imagine a heaven filled with Gods love
Like all God's creation we're all unique
Pray to our Lord if its answers you seek
Listen to the birds as they sing the Lords song
We're all God's creation, with him we belong
Never take for granted what tomorrow brings
And take a moment to listen when the bluebird sings

FOLLOW YOUR DREAM

Your life goes by fast, at least it does seem
So there's no time like now to realize your dream
The journey's long but there's only one way
Tomorrow will be a better day
Your journey may take many years
There'll be some laughter and perhaps a few tears
It's your destination that should be your goal
When your dream comes true you'll definitely know
When you reach your goal, don't stop there
There's more to conquer and more to share
If you are lucky and reach your goals
You can help others, there's lots of lost souls
If you are lonely reach out to a friend
They'll stick by you till the very end
With knowledge you gained you will not fail
Like a ship in the ocean, forever you'll sail

THE WIZARD

Who's that man behind that curtain?
He's says he's the wizard but I'm not certain
Before you trust him, trust your heart
Use your brain, that's a good place to start
Have the courage to make a decision
Be true to yourself, have a vision
You may be someone special indeed
You may be a person that's able to lead
You possess the passion in your heart
You may have talent in music or art
You'll find your niche, it just takes time
It may take years but that's no crime
As you mature you'll know yourself better
Some day you might even be a trend setter
Most important you must know who you are
You could be a budding superstar
You are very important, you have lots to give
Your future is clearer the longer you live
So when talking to the wizard remember one thing
You're probably smarter than that ding- a-ling
The last thing you tell him as you depart
What's important in life is the love in your heart

WHISKEY HILL

Back in the day, I remember it still
We lived in a town called Whiskey Hill
A blue collar town, the men they worked hard
The women were held in high regard
A gentle giant was my dad
Very seldom did I see him ever get mad
Our life was simple in Whiskey Hill
Ma stayed at home, dad worked at the mill
As hard as dad worked, so did my mother
Our town was small, we all knew each other
Ma and dad passed, and I since moved away
I now tell my children, we'll go there some day
Our life is now hectic, this I regret
Our life on the Hill, I'll never forget
It's been thirty years but I remember it still
Our peaceful life in Whiskey Hill

BEST DAY EVER

Life is too short, don't take it for granted
Life's like that flower you just planted
I have a wonderful life some people say
It's hard to remember my very best day
It could be when my two sons were born
Or when I wake up each early morn
I thought one day I had the answer
Until I met this boy battling cancer
As we talked for a while one thing became clear
This boy was heroic, he conquered his fears
His battle with cancer made him real strong
He said life is precious no matter how long
Each breath is a gift from our dear Lord
Wasting it is something we can't afford
I said to this very heroic young man
Tell me your best day if you can
He said he had many that were his best
But one day stood out from the rest
The doctor told him he was cancer free
He said that was the best day that ever could be
The little boy said the Lord heard his prayers
And he was blessed with a family who truly cares
From that day on each night I would pray
When there's a cure for cancer that'll be my best day

WISDOM

Does knowledge come from the books you read?
How many facts can you store in your head?
You can learn about life out on the street
A little of both would be a treat
I didn't learn much when I was in school
I was out playing football when I had homework to do
I should have listened more and respected my teacher
I should have paid attention to our preacher
Pay attention to detail, talk to somebody old
If you do these two things you'll be smarter I'm told
Older people have so much knowledge to give
Take their advice on how to live
What you do with your wisdom is the key
You can use it or waste it needlessly
Talk to young people, stay in touch
The difference between us isn't that much
Relaxing your mind could be the key
Meditation will help you stay stress free
As you get older you'll have wisdom to give
Pass it someone who just started to live
If we all give a little how great it would be
We'd all make decisions intelligently

ALL ALONE

It's a cold bitter night with snow on the ground
The sirens in the city are the only sounds
A warm dumpster to sleep in would be paradise
Any food in the garbage would be a welcome surprise
My life changed so fast it almost seems funny
I owned a house, a car and had lots of money
I had some bad luck, I bought stocks that were risky
Then I drowned myself in some very cheap whiskey
My family they left me but they're not to blame
I have lots of excuses but they're all pretty lame
I know there are others worse off than me
Who knows what the future has in store for me
From the streets you see life in a whole different light
And you better be tough, it's one hell of a fight
So I guess I'll take one day at a time
Stay out of trouble, don't commit any crimes
To every poor person climbing out of a hole
"They can take all your money, but they can't take your soul"

FACE IN THE CROWD

I can't remember the day of my birth
But I felt my dad's presence my first day on this earth
I can imagine him there with his five-o clock shadow
A proud pop he was as he bought my first rattle
My dad always said "be humble, my son"
But that was hard when I hit a home run
It was little league and the people cheered loud
But as I rounded the bases, I saw just one face in the crowd
I don't remember much as I reached third base
Except the proud look on my dad's face
It was my senior year on our high school team
When I looked in the stands, I saw my dad's face gleam
There was nobody else I'd rather please
If I had a bad game dad would put me at ease
He said "don't hang your head if you gave it your all"
Be proud young man and always stand tall
At every event my dad would be there
He loved and supported me, he really did care
It finally arrived, graduation day
I was valedictorian and I had plenty to say
As I got up to speak, I glanced through the crowd
I looked for dad, but he was nowhere to be found
As I gave my speech, I had this sick feeling
I couldn't look at the crowd, so I looked at the ceiling
Graduation was over but I didn't give a lick
As mom came over, she said "dad is very sick"
I went totally numb and from the school I fled
When I got to his room dad was in bed
I knew this was it my dad was dying
As he spoke to me, I couldn't stop crying
He said
I did the best I could, you made me so proud
I'll always be the face you see in the crowd
I'm your biggest fan and I love you so
And I'll always be sitting the very first row
I held my dad's hand as he slipped away
And I'll never forget the last words day would say

"someday you will have a son of your own
Be the face in the crowd so he won't feel alone
If you're lucky he'll grow up just like you
You'll love him, cherish him, and be proud of him too

A BIRDS EYE VIEW

The birds eye view at Flagler beach is really quite the sight
Children playing in the sand, kids are flying kites
The sands so orange from way up here, it's truly where it's at
Men are wearing speedos who really are too fat
The ladies take their clothes off, put on their skimpy suits
If they weren't three hundred pounds, they might be cute
I must find a bathroom I have to take a crap
I think I might just have to go upon this fellow's cap
He won't know where it came from as he looks up in the air
At least I didn't take a crap upon this fellow's hair
As I fly back home, I'm getting cold the darkness I do fear
I wave goodbye to fishermen as they fish off Flagler Pier!

PERCEPTION

There may be perception in this country song
But I assume my wife's cheating when she sneaks in at dawn
Her breath smells like whiskey as she crawls in our bed
She was with someone else, what else can be said
She's as cold as this late cold bitter night
My heart is breaking this just don't feel right
As she falls fast asleep, I lay in deep thought
I know that she's cheating does she care if she's caught
I light up a cigarette, my heart is racing
I get out of bed and I began pacing
Where did I go wrong, why this deception?
Is this all real, or is it perception?
As she lays there in bed it's an angel, I see
But it's the devil inside her that won't let us be
How do I compete with a man I don't know?
Should I pull out my gun or just let her go
When my angel wakes up with her bloodshot eyes
I'll look in them deeply and look for the lies
My heart will be breaking but she'll never know
I have a redneck heart, my feelings won't show
I'll just jump in my truck and head out west
Cause running away is what I do best
She can drink her tequila and stay out all night
I'll keep on driving till I feel alright
She can hurt someone else with her lies and deception
I know now our lives were just a perception

BACK TO NATURE

Some days I can feel it, it's in the air
There's beauty to be found everywhere
From birds singing songs up in the trees
To the beautiful color of bumble bees
The graceful butterfly that just flew by
Or the gliding hawk up in the sky
The sky is so blue no clouds to be found
This day's like a portrait, there's no need for sound
The carefree turtle, just strutting along
Not a worry in the world what could be wrong
The lake is so still, everyone's fishing
Catching that big one, everyone's wishing
I can smell the grass that had just been cut
It takes you out of that long winter rut
People are biking and jogging too
The children are visiting our neighborhood zoo
Everyone's smiling what a glorious day
The flowers are blooming in the month of May
As the sun goes down and day turns to night
The stars and the moon are a beautiful sight
As I look in the darkness, my mind starts to wander
The calmness and stillness make you ponder
The sun will rise in just a few hours
You can smell the dew upon the flowers
Nature is great there's so much to see
It picks up our spirit and sets your soul free
Just close your eyes don't say a word
Imagine you're flying just like a bird
No worries no problems to be found
The feisty wind is the only sound
As you're flying through the sky so blue
You'll have a different point of view!

STAN THE STUTTURING BIRD

His name was Stan the stuttering bird
His chirps were the first sounds each morning we heard
He'd stutter a tune about quarter to eight
He made sure we got up so we wouldn't be late
He was a star, he would sing alone
His pitch was perfect, he had a great tone
He lived in a tree up in a nest
Stuttering Stan always gave us his best
He could sing bass, or he could sing tenor
And he always attracted the opposite gender
Stuttering Stan could belt out a tune
He started his singing about the middle of June
One morning I didn't hear Stan anymore
Then I noticed he moved to the neighbor next door
I wondered if we had done something wrong
I missed our friend Stan and his beautiful songs
I loved the way stuttering Stan would rock
And wake us up without a clock
What did I do to chase him away?
We hope you come back to visit some day

WINTER

AS I glance outside it looks so cold
The snow's piled up along the road
It's a winter wonderland, a storybook scene
Winter's begun, the snow looks clean
The birds all flew south a month ago
They normally leave before the first snow
So I bundle up and venture outside
I get on board for a long winter ride
It's not a surprise, it comes every year
But we're never quite sure when the first flake will appear

CANCER CAN'T

Cancer can't take away your heart felt love
It comes from dear Jesus from heaven above
Cancer can't take away our souls
It can't take away our lofty goals
Cancer can't take away our smiles
It can't take away our unique styles
Cancer can't take away our passion
It can't take away our love for fashion
It can't take away how we feel
Our dreams for our future no matter how real
It can't take away how we care
Our sense of humor, so precious and rare
Cancer will try to keep us down
But it can never force us to wear a frown
It can take our energy but not our zest
It can't take away what we do best
Cancer can never take away our past
It's our memories we have that will forever last
It can't take away our spirit or strength
It's what we do in our life, not the length
It can try to create pain and sorrow
But it can't take away the hope for tomorrow
It can't take away our dignity
It can't make us sad or have self pity
It can't take away our special touch
Cancer doesn't have to be a crutch
Cancer can't take away our friends
Or the "Word" from the bible that the scripture sends
Cancer's in for a fight because we are resilient
Remember life is a Marathon, it isn't a sprint

MY HERO ANDREW

Going to camp is always a joy
Last year was special when I met this little boy
He was very funny and so very cool
He said "Don't call me Andy, my name is Andrew"
As the first day of camp came to an end
I knew I just made a special friend
It was nothing he said or nothing he had done
It was just being with Andrew was so much fun
When we arrive at camp we're all a little nervous
We all start to bond at the memorial service
Andrew was a comedian right from the start
I knew he'd hold a special place in my heart
From sleeping in bunk beds side by side
To going to the pool, or a horsy ride
As a counselor I've met doctors, lawyers and such
But the kids are the ones that taught me so much
It humbled me and made me a much better man
I'm really just trying to understand
When Andrew and I would get up to fish
Besides catching the big one I had this one wish
That we all could come back to this camp some day
And talk about the "cure" that took cancer away

Dedicated to every brave little girl or boy who had to endure
This horrible disease. You're an inspiration to us all and you are our "HERO"

A MOMENT IN TIME

Tic toc, tic toc
Wouldn't you like to stop the clock?
If time could stand still for a couple of years
We might be able to conquer our fears
We might slow down, we'd feel freer

Our bones wouldn't ache because we wouldn't grow old
If we stopped time during summer we'd never get cold
Our pets would live longer, we wouldn't be sad
We'd drive much slower, we wouldn't get mad
We would stay up late and sleep to noon
We could watch the stars and admire the moon
We could slow way down and not have to hurry
WE wouldn't be stressed, we'd never worry
We would have time to get in shape
There would be no use for video tape
I know this is just a dream of mine
But is having a dream really a crime
I know we can't stay young forever
It's nice to dream, I'll never say never

FOUR SEASONS OF LIFE

Like summer your young, everything shines
It really is the best of times
The sky is blue, the grass is green
Like your childhood years things are pure and clean
The days are longer, you can play all day
You have no problems, the world seems okay
When you find your first love, the world stands still
Like the heat in the summer, it will test your will
But like your first love summer comes to an end
You never believe that your heart will mend
The trees so green turn colors in fall
It's like changes in life, I do recall
You're in the autumn of life, you realize now
How you got there, you don't know how
Like winter, you're older, bitter and cold
Keep the warmth in your heart and you'll never feel old
When the long winter ends it finally is spring
If you listen closely you will hear the birds sing
Your problems like snow are melting away
You can't wait for morning to start a new day

RAISIN IN THE SUN

I'm just a young grape hanging on this vine
My goal in life is to be in a fine wine
I hang here all day and it sure does get hot
I wish I could move to a shadier spot
I shouldn't complain, it don't do any good
I'll just hang out here like I know I should
Someday soon I'll be picked from this vine
I could end up in an expensive wine
It could take years to get to a store
I know I must age and ferment some more
The older I get the better I'll taste
So I guess all this time wasn't a waste
I do get bored hanging around
But I must stay perky, I can't get down
I might end up in some musty wine cellar
By then I'll be a pretty old feller
I think I'd be good in a nice Merlot wine
I'd be at a restaurant where couples dine
It could be a very romantic night
With me at your table it would make it just right
Some nights I wish upon a star
I don't end up in a jelly jar
I do have nightmares on occasion
I'm a wrinkled old grape that turned into a raison
So as I get older I should get picked soon
I thank god I'm a grape and not an old prune

ULTIMATE WARRIOR #68

Think in your mind of the prototype guard
If you are a Buffalo Bills fan don't think too hard
Our line was weak, it needed a cure
So the Bills drafted Joe DeLamielleure
He was the ultimate warrior, a gentleman too
He made holes so big you could drive a bus through
They were the "Electric Company", they turned on the "Juice"
When Joe D blocked O.J. would turn loose
Joe would play tough, but he would play fair
He was very humble, that really is rare
A blue collar guy, he brought his lunch pail to work
He felt playing was a privilege, being a pro was a perk
With O.J., Braxton and our QB Fergie
Joe blocked the likes of Butkus and Bergy
He was the best guard, pound for pound
They ran behind Joe to get the first down
With Saban as coach they always played hard
Joe would scrap for every last yard
There was no quit in Joe, he'd fight till the end
It's how he lived life, a great message to send
As great as he was, he's in the Hall of Fame
Family came first, footballs just a game
Joe was athletic, he could play any sport
You should see how he moved on the racquetball court
I think we all knew right from the start
He'd forever be in all Bills fans hearts

BUFFALO'S TIME

Buffalo's excited, you ask what is up
We think we can win the Stanley cup
Forget "No goal" or Norwood's "Wide right"
This time we have our prize in sight
Our team is focused and the message they send
No "Music city miracle" at the end
Our goaltending's great, our forwards are fast
Our bad luck is over, that's all in the past
Bring it on Flyers, you aren't so tough
You won't out coach us, we have Lindy Ruff
We're from Buffalo but don't shed a tear
We serve chicken wings with Genesee beer
If you're not with us yet, still not believing
You better hop on board, this bandwagon's leaving
This is the real thing, it's not a charade
We'll see you at the victory parade
This could be what finally cures our ills
A championship for the Sabres and hopefully the Bills

**(Dedicated to all the loyal Buffalo fans who endured many years
Of broken hearts and unfulfilled dreams)**

DON'T BE AFRAID

Don't be afraid to stand up and be loud
When you accomplish a feat, be humble yet proud
If the music is playing go out there and dance
Life is a gamble, you must take a chance
Who says you're too old to go back to school
Education will never make you a fool
You must taste that the fruit that life dishes out
There's so much to do, make each moment count
You should swim that lake or run that race
You must not delay, there's no time to waste
There's lots of excuses, we could count the ways
In life we only have so many days
Don't feel defeated before you start
It's not the size of your muscles, it's the size of your heart
Imagine the impossible then follow your dream
It's not half as hard as it may seem
Some people say that you're too old
You're as young as you feel, that's what I am told
It's not how you finish, it's the journey you take
So, embrace the world each day you're awake

THE WISEMAN SAID

Never lie to a man in a suit
Don't ever think that you're too cute
Make sure you are wearing clean underwear
In poker don't bluff with a pair
Don't ever believe you're too smart
Never put the horse before the cart
Don't ever refer to a woman as mam
Don't ever confuse a sheep and a ram
Don't ever forget your anniversary
Buy her flowers from her favorite nursery
Let your boss think he's always right
Only eat snow if it is white
Don't shop for a gift at a Goodwill store
Don't talk too much, you become a bore
Train your dog not to jump
When you're playing pinnacle, know when to trump
Never write a check you can't cover
Don't ever think you're a hot Latin lover
Don't grow your hair longer than your sisters
Never break your water blisters
Eat lots of veggies and you will live long
And never be afraid to sing your "Song"

WHAT I MISS

I've been here for fifty years or so
There are things I miss from years ago
Buying sneakers for two bucks
Playing with my Tonka trucks
I remember being five and going to school
Dressed in new clothes I thought I looked cool
I remember the first time I bought my lunch
And my sweetheart Sue who I liked a bunch
Then came first grade and school got much harder
I tried my best, but didn't feel much smarter
Grammar school was just a blur
The years flew by, that's for sure
Then came high school, what a blast
The years flew by way too fast
I wish I could have those years back
I'd do things different, I'd know how to act
Days seemed happier and simpler back then
If I could go back here's the message I'd send
Live every day, don't worry about tomorrow
Enjoy your friends don't dwell on your sorrow
We sang about war, we prayed for peace
Riots and violence is what I liked least
But the thing I miss the very most
Was Grandma's jam, and my mother's toast

NO FEAR

When I was a child all I would hear
Were the things in life I was supposed to fear?
It stopped me from doing what I wanted to do
My accomplishments were small and very few
When I played football and entered the game
I feared if I failed, could I get through the shame
Coach said, "You must taste failure before success
All you can do is your very best"
If Tom Edison feared that he might not be right
We'd be sitting in the dark without any light
Imagine Knute Rockne saying "We can't win this game"
There'd be no mystique at Notre Dame
I saw a classmate they said wouldn't succeed
He made it big, because he believed
The word "Can't" is a word I never use
If you don't try to win, you're going to lose
Imagine not landing a man on the moon
Or Walt Disney not trying to draw a cartoon
The belief in yourself is a very big part
Mix in some knowledge and add some heart
Don't listen to others, follow your dream
Others may follow and join your team
So go conquer something you never have done
Have no fear and have lots of fun

PREACHER RAY

I was riding my bike to Daytona Beach
The ocean so close you feel you can reach
The day was humid, the sun beating down
It was high tide, the ocean was loud
I rode down the ocean, twenty two miles
There were surfers, joggers and people with smiles
I got to Daytona at half past three
I found a comfortable bench under a tree
Starring at the ocean I fell fast asleep
I started to dream, I was in a deep sleep
I then heard this man, he was talking to me
When he touched my shoulder I felt serenity
He asked "Who is Jesus", I told him my savior
He then asked if Jesus could do me a favor
I told this nice man that I was Okay
But for my cousin with Leukemia could we please pray
He had tattooed arms, he was a big man
I could feel his passion when he shook my hand
He asked what I needed as he walked away
I told him I want a grandchild some day
Something told me he was an angel from above
I could feel the Lords presence and all his love
I sat on the bench for an hour or so
Would my cousin be cured, only Jesus would know?
I believe in Miracles and I felt one that day
There was a reason I was there, to meet Preacher Ray

BAD NEWS, GOOD NEWS

If I need some sorrow I just turn on the news
It's like going to a bar where they're singing the blues
Some people seem to thrive on that stuff
But day in, day out it gets pretty tough
Bad news sells and people want more
A fire, a robbery at a Ma and Pa's store
While the fire is blazing there's crime on the street
A guy gets shot for not giving up his seat
Enough is enough, I need some good news
I'm tired of people breaking the rules
Take the guns off the streets, put the criminals away
It's time for good people to have a say
Let kids be kids but pay attention
If not they could end up in detention
If you steal from someone, you will pay a price
It's not that hard to be honest or nice
The news I crave is a cure for cancer
For each child who suffers I pray for an answer
When I turn on the news I'd love a good story
Instead I see scenes that are bloody and gory
Let's stay positive, show our kids the way
And maybe our news will be better some day

MY MISTAKE

My boss called me in because I made a mistake
I asked him just how many does that make
He replied only one but that's one too many
I said show me a person who doesn't make any
A hard working person would know what I mean
Our biggest mistake we haven't yet seen
You pointed it out and that's quite all right
I know I messed up so there will be no fight
I may be wrong but mistakes are corrected
Ask any politician who has been elected
Correct me once and it won't happen again
Making one mistake isn't a sin
I think that's why erasers were made
And like your memory in time it will fade
Having said all this thank you so much
Coming from you I am truly touched
I know you are smart and can do no wrong
So feel free to reticule me when the chance comes along
Now I think I'll go home to my beautiful wife
And my cute little boy, the best "Mistake" of my life

A CHILD AT HEART

I'm a child at heart and will be forever
That don't make me bad or any less clever
I just see things in a different way
I live my life and do as I may
I never take myself real serious
Sometimes I laugh until I'm delirious
I block out misery and try to have fun
I like my hotdogs without any bun
I'm not too formal, I can't set a table
I don't count calories or read the food label
You can't get me mad, you're wasting your time
I don't watch the news, I'm sick of the crime
I am your worst nightmare at a funeral home
My eulogies read like a funny poem
I'm comic relief for family and friends
I hope my sense of humor never ends
I may not be the sharpest tool in the shed
But I can make decisions, I can use my head
This is my life and I'll do as I choose
In the midst of the day I may take a snooze
I don't worry much about having no money
I talk to my accountant, he is pretty funny
I don't want stress, my hair may fall out
I'd rather stay positive then sit there and pout
So do me a favor and dance with me
Because tomorrow will soon be history

HERE FOR A WHILE

Do it today, don't wait till tomorrow
Cheer up, be happy, and forget all your sorrow
Get rid of that frown, put on your best smile
We're only here for such a short while
If you want to go skydiving, do it today
If you have the will you find the way
Did you promise your son you'd take him fishing?
Did you go on that cruise or are you still wishing
Life is too short, time really flies
There's beauty around, just open your eyes
Tomorrow's not promised so live every day
We should not worry what people may say
This is your life, live it with zest
Whatever you do give it your best
The journey of life could end any time
You won't conquer that mountain if you never climb
You work all your life for status and wealth
What's important in life is family and health
Your spiritual life is important too
Jesus is with us whatever we do
The peace inside you is a good feeling
The sky's the limit, there is no ceiling
So tonight take a moment to say a prayer
God will listen because he truly does care

SAY IT TODAY

Have you told someone lately to have a great day?
Did you mean it or was it just something to say
Did you thank the crossing guard for keeping kids safe?
Did you tell the homeless person, "Keep the faith?"
Have you told your kids how proud you are?
Did you wish upon a shooting star?
Tomorrows not promised, who knows our fate
Say it today before it's too late
Thank mom and dad for giving you life
Give thanks every day for your beautiful wife
Give thanks to the firefighters who put their life on the line
Let an elderly person go ahead of the line
Pray your community leaders remain to be strong
Call a sick friend, don't wait too long
Tell a soldier it's them you're praying for
The ones at home and the ones at war
Thank our dear Lord, tell him you care
Try living your life through love and through prayer

A LITTLE BIT CRAZY

When somebody tries to figure me out
I don't let them know what I'm thinking about
I am energetic, yet at times I am lazy
I'm sometimes sane and sometimes crazy
I keep people guessing, I keep them off guard
Figuring me out can be very hard
I don't care if someone thinks I am strange
I can be in plain sight, yet out of range
I don't want to be your best friend
All good friendships come to an end
Don't talk to me, I won't respond
My goal in life isn't to bond
Being crazy suits me just fine
The difference between sanity and insanity is a fine line
The only one I trust is my golden retriever
Unconditional love, I am a believer
He understands the way I think
He knows what I mean when I give him a wink
I have no enemies, because I don't have a friend
By now people know the message I send
If I don't get too close I can't get hurt
If I see a nice girl I won't even flirt
I'm not even interested in making small talk
I'd much rather take my dog for a walk
So if you come up and say hi to me
I say "Back off Jack", or its trouble you'll see

JESUS, MY ROLE MODEL

He never scored a touchdown or hit a home run
Jesus has been my role model since my life begun
He never won a Super Bowl or Stanley Cup
In track the hurdles he did not jump
He's the ultimate role model, he's loved by us all
He'll pick you up if you happen to fall
With Jesus on my side I never feel alone
It matters not the possessions I own
He's a scholar, a mentor, my best friend
If my heart breaks, he will help it mend
In the sand his footprints I cannot see
But I know at times he carried me
I continue to pray and ask for his love
He is shining down from heaven above

CHARISMA

It's just a word, but it means a lot
It's something you have or haven't got
You cannot buy it no matter how much you spend
It's not something you borrow or something you lend
I like to refer to it as the big "C"
It's one of those things that's totally free
As far as charisma I can only assume
You know who has it when they enter the room
People take notice, there's a special glow
They don't say a word but everyone knows
They always have friends, they're never alone
There's confidence in their voice, it's in their tone
You can use charisma for good or bad
You can make people happy, you can make people sad
It's a gift they have, no return receipt
It seems to grow the more people they meet
You can make babies laugh, you can make grownups cry
You can be quite convincing, nobody knows why
Count your blessings if you have the big "C"
Just like money, it doesn't grow on a tree

EDDIE ELEVATOR

My Job's not exciting it's really a bore
All I do is get people from floor to floor
Just push my buttons and watch me work
But only push one, don't be a jerk
If you're running late call someone who cares
If you need to lose weight please use the stairs
Deodorant's nice, please do not smell
And don't look around, we can all tell
What's said in here stays in here
I don't gossip, you have nothing to fear
Don't bring in large items, I hate all that weight
If you go over the limit you could have bad fate
I work very hard year after year
All I ask is maintenance to oil my gears
I work in the cold, I work in the heat
I don't need much rest, I don't need to eat
I'm very low maintenance, it's not attention I seek
I'm very low key, I'm actually a geek
I know I'm no escalator, but you could ride me all day
You won't get lost, you don't have to pay
I even speak for the visually impaired
I don't ask for much, just someone who cares
Please don't come on with dirty shoes
And don't come every morning singing the blues
I may look tough with all my gear
I do have feelings and I do have tears
So next time you take me to the very top floor
Please try to nice or don't use me any more

TURNING THIRTY

You were wild in your teens, somehow you got through
You partied in your twenties, you thought you were cool
Your life was exciting, never a bore
You'd dance all night and never get sore
Now that you're thirty you slowed way down
Those days are over, carousing around
Instead you stay home and watch TV
Your Friday night beverage is a cup of tea
You destroyed your body long enough
You thought you were invincible but you weren't that tough
You start to stock up on vapor rub
You notice your hair falling out in the tub
If you're not married do it quick
You'll need someone to nurse you when you get sick
You can't be vain, this you should know
Don't worry about your looks, turn the lights down low
Your metabolism will start to slow down
If you eat all that junk food, you'll put on the pounds
But don't fret my friend, it isn't all bleak
You'll be fine if it's happiness that you seek
You may have more wrinkles than an old cotton shirt
But you do have charisma and you know how to flirt
Don't worry about the gray that's now in your hair
You have bigger problems that you will bear
So if there's any advice I might give it to you
Be true to yourself, and you'll always be cool

A WONDERFUL DAY

Have you ever had a perfect day?
Nothing goes wrong, things go your way
The sky is blue, it's eighty degrees
The birds are singing up in the trees
You're feeling good, like a million bucks
What did you do to deserve this luck?
Look up in the sky at each shining star
They look so close yet they are so far
You have good karma, your glass is half full
You're as sharp as a tack and strong as a bull
Are you dreaming or is this for real
Nothing goes wrong, you like how you feel
You thank your dear Lord for this wonderful day
There's one more thing you'd like to say
"Dear Lord I know you care about me
I have a friend who cannot see
I'd trade this day to give him sight
I know it's not simple as black and white
Could you let him see his beautiful wife?
And help him have a normal life
Thank you for letting me have my say
And thank you for my beautiful day"

GOING FISHING

I'm going fishing, have to find my poles
The fish are biting as the cold stream flows
I set my alarm for five o' clock
My alarm clock's loud, I sleep like a rock
I make sure my truck has enough gas
In' a couple hours I'll be fishing for bass
It's dark in the morning as I start on my journey
I have to pick up my good friend Ernie
As he gets in my truck he looks half asleep
I let him rest, I don't make a peep
We're almost there, I can feel my heart pound
The running stream is my favorite sound
As we get on our gear and head down the stream
I look at my friend and see his eyes gleam
It's always a blast to fish with my friend
I wish this day never would end
Two hours go by, we both caught two fish
This would hardly fill a dinner dish
But all of a sudden we got some good luck
We put them on ice in the back of my truck
We caught a few bass and plenty of trout
But the fun are the stories we'll be talking about
As we head home I'm certainly glad
About the fish we caught and the fun we had
But reality sets in as our fishing trip ends
When's our next trip, I guess it depends
When we get home with all our fish
Going back to the stream is my number one wish

BIG CHEESE

I live in the dairy, life is a breeze
Everyone knows me as the "Big Cheese"
The temperature's great, not too hot or too cold
I'm on sale this week so I'll likely be sold
I miss all my friends as they leave the store
It makes me sad, I won't see them no more
I'm an American cheese, not sharp or cheddar
Sometimes I feel they think they are better
Life in the dairy is total bliss
I have friends who are Romano, and friends who are Swiss
And yes there is someone who makes my heart flutter
She's a beautiful slender stick of butter
While I really don't know her I can tell she has style
She's not like the others who live down the isle
If I saw her on popcorn it would make my heart melt
Sometimes I wish she knew how I felt
I'm pretty good looking, this I must boast
Imagine us both on piece of toast
Last night I had this terrible dream
I dreamt she was dating vanilla whipped cream
I was really sleeping like a rock
When I woke up they were rotating stock
When they rotated us later the timing seemed right
They put her up front, plainly in sight
Just then a customer put her in their cart
I felt like Swiss cheese, there was a hole in my heart
But then they also picked up me
I guess you can say it was meant to be
We're a match made in heaven but there was this small hitch
We both ended up on a "Grilled Cheese Sandwich"

"PLAY ME A TUNE"

There is nothing as sad as an old country song
When a cowboy tells how his life has gone wrong
His wife had just left him, his dog up and died
He had a best friend until he found he had lied
When you hear his sad story you're as blue as can be
Sometimes I feel this song could be me
I put on some Manilow with that Congo beat
Or Jimmy Buffett to feel tropical heat
At times I listen to the blues
Imagine Bourbon Street with a bottle of booze
A nice slow ballad on a Saturday night
With a beautiful woman can make it just right
There is some music that frees the soul
Like the Beach Boys singing Kokomo
There was no one like Joplin, I've been told
If you like the Beatles there's Abbey Road
The song Harlem Nocturne, I can still hear that sax
You don't need your speakers turned to the max
From Elvis, the Beatles to the Dave Clark Five
These Icons helped keep Rock and Roll alive
If you like jazz there's Louis Armstrong
Somewhere over the Rainbow was Judy Garland's best song
There are songs that really touch your heart
And others that really tear you apart
There's patriotic songs in "Two thousand one
You can't find a dry eye when these songs are sung
There is one thing you must know for sure
To mend a broken heart, music's the cure

UNDER THE RAINBOW

Under the rainbow up in the sky
Are where wishes come true and bluebirds fly
There's a wizard of Oz, so smart and witty
In a mythical place they called Emerald City
If I had but one wish I'd like him to answer
I'd ask him to cure each child that had cancer
They don't need a brain, these kids are so smart
They possess so much love, they don't need a heart
They have so much courage that goes without saying
They just need good health, that's what we're all praying
You helped the tin man, the lion, and scarecrow too
Please cure childhood cancer if it's the last thing you do
If you found the cure, it would be worth the wait
These kids don't deserve this horrible fate
Oh, powerful wizard we know that you care
No more chemo, radiation or losing their hair
You have the passion to find cancers cure
Please help these brave children, so precious and pure
We don't ask for riches or personal wealth
We just ask that these children all have good health
Camp Good Days is like the "Great Emerald City"
It's a magical place, there's no time for pity
So like the mythical wizard maybe some way
Our doctors could cure childhood cancer someday

BRICK WALL- PROFILES IN COURAGE

They said I had cancer at thirteen years old
My futures uncertain I've always been told
One day my dad said my son you stand tall
We'll beat this disease, we'll knock down this brick wall
I didn't understand what dad and mom meant
I faced each obstacle each place that I went
There was no time for crying, we had one job to do
We'll knock down this wall, we'll see this thing through
The brick wall was sturdy, it was very strong
But I had lots of time, I planned to live long
One brick at a time, we would find the answer
I told mom and dad we will beat this cancer
So we kicked out these bricks over the years
There were so many hurdles, there were laughter and tears
That wall that seemed sturdy and appeared to be strong
Was no match for the courage I had all along
We kicked out each brick, it started to crack
And the good friends I had all had my back
Mom, dad and I all did our part
This wall could not beat what we had in our heart
Sure it was hard but we fought every day
That last brick that fell took my cancer away
You would think that this journey would have been sad
But I see it much different thanks to my mom and dad
How lucky was I to knock down that wall
The pain I endured I can hardly recall
I'm now a young man with kids of my own
They know of the wall now that they're grown
I taught them about courage, so they'd never quit
The things we conquer, you must never forget
So goodbye brick wall you now must depart
You were very strong but so was my heart

MY HOT ROD COUGER

When I was young and a little bit bold
I put my Cougar on the road
With leather seats and a stick on the floor
It attracted the girls, who could ask for more
The engine purred like a pussycat
The view was great from where I sat
My Cougar was built in sixty nine
The color was burgundy wine
I'd pick up my friends and we'd go cruising
Life was great though a little confusing
Then one cold and blusterous night
I drove my car with all its might
My tires hit ice up on the hill
For about thirty seconds my life stood sill
I had no control, my car was swerving
I gripped the wheel, it was unnerving
How we survived I'll never know
My Cougar was smashed, we had to be towed
We were going to a party that Saturday night
We were told the girls were out of sight
As the doctor stitched me I said to my friend
The night was young, why should it end
We went to the party and it didn't take long
We forgot all that happened, nothing seemed wrong
I pray my Cougar is in car heaven
All polished and clean with the engine revving'
I guess the moral of the story I just told
Don't drive your car when it's icy and cold
But if something happens it isn't the end
Just go to the party with your best friend

A SHINING STAR

Don't be afraid to hit that high note
This song's about you, it's your life you wrote
Look to the heavens as the sun shines on you
It's time to move on and start anew
The lord gave you talent, don't be afraid
Today is your day, a star is made
Belt out those lyrics, they'll come from your heart
Your songs are unique like a good piece of art
Be true to yourself, give your songs soul
Singing to the world should be your goal
You sing like an angel from heaven above
You do have an aura, a voice people love
You're young and talented, you will go far
An American idol is who you are
Everyone loves you, the young and the old
You must take your music and hit the road
On your path to stardom you will have some bumps
But you must move on and take your lumps
The sky is the limit to where you can go
Your fans will be rocking at your first show
The world is your stage, you'll do very well
Where this will take you it's too soon to tell
It's not about your destination
Your journey will be a celebration
Don't ever forget who you are
You shine so bright, you're a rising star

SALUTING THE FOURTH

I can't recall the last time I was sober
Maybe September or early October
I enjoy drinking, don't ask me why
I'm drinking today, it's the Fourth of July
Sometimes I wish I could find a cure
The last couple years have been a blur
I'm not depressed, I just like the taste
But I don't drink a bottle, I drink the whole case
I wish I could tell you that it makes me feel better
The one thing it does is make my face redder
I wake up with flashbacks that happened last night
When I look in the mirror it's a hideous sight
For that brief moment I swear I'm done drinking
Then my friends all say, what the hell are you thinking?
At closing time the girls don't look better
But who am I to say, I'm no trendsetter
I know every bartender by their first name
They all say they're happy that I came
I am a guzzler, not a slow sipper
I am considered a generous tipper
Everyone calls me the life of the party
I tell a good joke, my laugh is real hardy
I don't have a car, I don't drink and drive
I guess that's the reason I still am alive
I do go to church, it's the Lord that I fear
If I make it to heaven I pray there is beer
So that's my story and that being said
I have a terrible headache and must go to bed

HAPPY HOUR

The weekend's over, it's back to work
The coffee's ready, I hear it perk
The creamer smells a little sour
I think last night my fridge lost power
My wife is yelling, it's six in the morning
I look outside, it just started pouring
Mondays are always a little rough
Friday can't get here soon enough
That's the day I can loosen the old collar
It's finally here, "HAPPY HOUR"
It doesn't much matter if I had a bad week
At happy hour it's fun that I seek
We work all week to pay our bills
I saved some money to cure my ills
Salsa, margaritas and Corona beer
Makes life seem better and my focus more clear
It's only one night for a couple of hours
But it's nice to stop and smell the flowers
When life gets hectic we must slow down
With a few whiskey sours you'll lose that frown
At happy hour everyone's your friend
I can't wait to Friday to do it again
Everyone bonds, there's no social classes
We drink from bottles, who needs glasses
For a couple of hours we don't have to rough it
We're in Margaretville with Jimmy Buffet
So put on your sandals and your flowered shirt
Put all your friends on special alert
It's Friday afternoon and I can hardly wait
Those Corona's are cold and the tacos taste great"

GARDEN OF LOVE

Imagine a garden filled with love
And it was blessed by our Lord from heaven above
It's a place to visit for peace and compassion
You could wear what you want, no one cares about fashion
The sun always shines, it's always so bright
The bluebirds here are a beautiful sight
The fruit can be picked right from the trees
You can eat the sweet honey made by the bees
You'll never hear anyone ever complain
The plants are green though there's not much rain
There are no wars, no droughts or starvation
It seems like everyone is on vacation
There are lions and bears but they're tender and mild
Even the tigers are gentle, not wild
There's a beach in the garden with crystal white sand
There's a tiki bar and a Jamaican band
People are smiling everywhere
There's no more anguish, there's no more despair
Everyone's equal, we're all treated the same
Everyone's welcome, they're happy you came
If there's work to be done they all chip in
People play games but don't care if they win
Everyone here has a good heart
They help their neighbors, they all do their part
I pray someday this garden I see
And I pray I'm there for eternity

REAL WORTH

I'm fresh out of cash, my gas tank is low
My mortgage is due in a day or so
Prices are rising, our pay stays the same
Staying above water is our only aim
I do use credit but I hate when it's due
I'd love to save money but don't have a clue
My cash flow is sick, it's on life support
The best way for money would land me in court
I'm playing lotto, but I never win
I'd love to invest but I need cash to begin
I shouldn't complain, I still have my health
Is it a sin to dream about wealth?
I take empty bottles back to the store
I count on this money like never before
When I go shopping I get depressed
I spend more money and come home with less
Is it me or are we all in the same boat
Are we all just trying to stay afloat?
I'm not selfish and it's not very funny
When the church basket's passed I have no money
I guess I am lucky, I have a good life
Two beautiful boys, a dog and a wife
I try not to worry, I live day to day
It's hard to pay bills on what I get paid
For richer or poorer, through sickness and health
I'll live a good life, my family's my wealth

CAN'T KEEP YOU DOWN

You feel the world upon your shoulders
The weight so great, like two huge boulders
But you refuse to be sad or wear a frown
You pick yourself up they can't keep you down
The Lord only gives you what you can handle
He's the eternal flame upon your candle
When it rains it pours or so they say
But the sun will come up the very next day
You were never afraid of an honest day's work
Your responsibilities you never did shirk
When life got tough and threw you a curve
You got much stronger, you had more nerve
You became outspoken, you were no longer meek
It was truth and respect that you would seek
What's important in life are friends and compassion
Don't be impressed by money or fashion
You always try hard, you do your best
You realize that life is a tough test
You won't go through life trouble free
How you handle adversity is the key
You surround yourself with a positive force
You try to stay focused and stay the course
No matter what people happen to say
They can't keep you down, no how, no way

SPRING TIME

Winter is over as we watch the snow melt
Springs beauty can be seen and also felt
The sun seems brighter and the chill is gone
If you listen closely you'll hear a bird song
The grass is greener, the nights are cool
The clouds are sparse, the sky is blue
People come out and live once more
Our aches go away, we don't feel as sore
The trees that were bare now have leaves
It's nice to know we can wear short sleeves
The brooks and streams are once again running
Some of the scenery is once again stunning
You can fish in the lake on your canoe
You can visit the animals at the zoo
Wildlife comes out this time of year
If you walk in the woods you might see some deer
With the long winter over we get back some pep
You might even notice a jump in your step
The lilies and tulips are out of the ground
The crickets at night are a beautiful sound
Spring has arrived and it gives us all hope
With days much brighter we feel we can cope

COLD WINTER MORNING

It was a cold winter morning, the wind was blowing
The sky was gray, it just started snowing
It was a perfect day to stay in bed
Should I go to work, or stay home instead
It was an easy decision but it had to be made
So I called in sick and in bed I laid
I thought how I'd sleep the day away
It was zero outside, a frigid day
I later made coffee, it taste so good
In my wood burning stove I threw in some wood
It was toasty inside but I had to get out
I'd soon be freezing, there was no doubt
I bundled up and walked out the door
I had to go to the grocery store
The birds looked frozen as they tried to fly
If my tears wouldn't freeze I'd probably cry
I don't like the cold, I should live in the south
The wind I so fierce I can't open my mouth
It's eighty out somewhere but it's zero out here
It seems we hibernate half of the year
I know some people who love the snow
But these long cold winters can take a toll
I can't really jog, I just slip and slide
I'm not really running, I just sort of glide
Just give me some sunshine and a nice cold beer
Goodbye cold winter, I'm out of here
No more grey skies, no more snow
"Hello Carolina, goodbye Buffalo"

THE WONDER YEARS

The year was nineteen fifty four
Life was simpler, values meant more
Dad worked hard, we were raised by our mother
If dad lost his job, he'd find another
Weekends were great, we'd finally see dad
These were the best times our family had
Sunday's at church we'd wear our best
Sunday's back then were a day of rest
The sixties came and it got pretty wild
We had the Vietnam War and the flower child
People were mellow, it could be the drugs
Most people were friendly, there were lots of hugs
The seventies came, it was the end of the war
Most had good jobs, who could ask for more
People got married and lived in the burbs
People were healthier, they were into their herbs
Women were working, they got out of the house
Divorce was more common, they didn't need their spouse
The eighties came and seemed like a blur
Aids was spreading, there wasn't a cure
In the nineties our money didn't go as far
Most of us drove an old rusty car
But things were great in Buffalo
We went to our very first Super Bowl
Two thousand came with lots of hope
Most people were trying to basically cope
In two thousand one they attacked our Twin Towers
Now it's time to reflect, and smell the flowers
Our world today is a much different place
We must once again become one human race

JOURNEY

Life is a journey with an occasional surprise
You are on the path to paradise
Temptations are plenty but you must stay the course
The Lord will guide you, he'll be your force
You'll get your help from heaven above
Just reach out to God for guidance and love
The power of love will get you through
Listen to Jesus, he is here for you
Life's journey is long, some days you will wander
Getting to heaven is what you must ponder
God's angels will help you along the way
Your tomorrow will be a better day
Don't forget to stop and smell the flowers
There's beauty around and it's all ours
Temptations are great, the rewards are few
Trust your heart and common sense too
Your knowledge will grow along the way
Use it wisely or a price you will pay
Care for the elderly and teach the young
Your life will have meaning when it's all said and done
At the end of this path you will see the light
That's when heavens gates will be in your sight
It's here where the Lord will take you home
And in his garden you will forever roam
When Jesus embraces you how happy you'll be
You'll sing alleluia and your soul will be free

A NEW YEAR

It's another year and I can't complain
But as I look closer it's a little insane
The violence must stop, we can't have any more
We must shelter our homeless and must stop all wars
We must cure cancer, no children should die
I can't stand to see one more parent cry
We all must get stronger and learn to cope
We must elect people who give us hope
We must have vision and meet all our goals
We must look deep into our souls
We must trust God, he does have a plan
And do not forget he's our biggest fan
We must help others who aren't as strong
We must teach our kids right from wrong
Life is a privilege, not a right
Have faith and keep Jesus in your sight
We must not see color, we're one human race
We must help the needy and problems they face
We must look for good, not the bad
We must stay positive and not be sad
People with money should share their wealth
Money and fortune can't buy your health
We must cherish each moment, live every day
Don't forget the departed each night that we pray
If you feel lost take the Lords hand
On your own two feet you'll once again stand
Remember these things and you'll have a great year
You'll be a much better person with nothing to fear

SMALL TOWN USA

My home is small time USA
These small town values should help some day
I'm so proud to be a small town guy
I can still smell mom's sweet apple pie
The corner store is where we would shop
We have one traffic light where people would stop
Our small town church is where we would pray
Our small hotel is where our guests stay
We have one barber shop where we would all go
We know where it is by the barber shop pole
We have a family diner, it's where we all eat
It's also a place where we like to meet
We have Joe the mechanic at our only gas station
I don't recall Joe ever taking a vacation
We have strong beliefs and good ideals
It's hard to explain how a small town feels
We stick together, we're all very close
Our love for each other is what I love most
There's only one factory in our small town
What a beautiful sunset when the sun goes down
We have just one sheriff but that's quite enough
He is a gentle man, but he could be tough
We have one politician, he is our mayor
We see him each year at our county fair
At this fair we'd all be once a year
We'd eat corn on the cob, drink homemade beer
I guess what I'm really trying to say
I'll love my hometown 'till my very last day
If you pass through our town please stay a while
The welcome mat's out and so is our smile

MAN OF STEEL, HEART OF GOLD

There was nobody like my old man
You knew he was tough when you shook his hand
He worked in the steel mill eighty hours a week
Unlike my mom he wasn't meek
He was a mountain of a man and lots of fun
I was very proud to be his son
I never saw my father cry
'Till my mother left us last July
I wish I knew how my dad felt
As tough as he was I saw his heart melt
Mom told us she was moving away
She didn't love dad, she could not stay
Dad really aged, he looked twenty years older
He never complained, there was a lot on his shoulders
Dad promised he'd do the best he could
He loved us so much, I knew he would
We all helped out, dad was proud
Our family got closer, this I found
Years flew by, things got much better
Then one day, my dad got this letter
It was from my mom and the letter read
I love you and miss you my mother said
Tell the children I'm sorry but I had to leave
It was for the best I believe
I don't have long, maybe a week
It's your love and forgiveness that I seek
I'll soon be with Jesus, this I hope
I know you are strong, I know you will cope
I know for years we've been apart
But I always kept you close in my heart"
When dad finished the letter we had a good cry
This was mom's way of saying goodbye
Dad tried to cope the best that he can
This man of steel was a special man

PUT ON A SMILE

People today are in a bad mood
Driving to work people are rude
There's road construction mile after mile
I think I'll be stuck for quite a while
People are cranky, I don't understand
We're all just doing the best we can
Staying upbeat has been my style
I try to stay positive and put on a big smile
To pout or be angry just isn't my way
When I meet a stranger I say have a great day
Things will get better, just wait and see
Life is too short for both you and me
Being nice to people is easy to do
You'll feel much better and happier too
We're going to be here for quite a while
So go through life with your beautiful smile
You'll be surprised how different you'll feel
Helping out others is a big deal
When you treat others with love and respect
You'll notice a difference, you'll see the effect
Your smile can work wonders, don't be afraid
Don't let God's love wither and fade
We all are Lords children, he loves us the same
We shouldn't point fingers, there's no one to blame
Helping others is where it begins
Instead of a frown, put on a nice grin
So next time a stranger comes up to you
Put on a nice smile and say how do you do
Help spread happiness and always be kind
Life will be brighter, this you will find

THE OLD ROCKPILE

It was the mid-sixties, Namath's a Jet
I still smell the hotdogs, how can I forget
We had season tickets behind a huge pole
We sat really high, the eightieth row
We were Buffalo Bills fans through and through
For the Bills we all bled red, white and blue
We sat through the rain, we sat through the snow
We were proud to be living in Buffalo
The colder it got the better for the Bills
The other team was cold and getting the chills
There was lots of yelling and plenty of beers
And when the Bills lost there were plenty of tears
They played for the game, not the money
With the players today that seems sort of funny
If you parked your car or parked your truck
The price for parking was only a buck
There was no tailgating, we just went to the game
We were one big family, it just isn't the same
I remember Dawson, Blanda and Broadway Joe
Miami was always our toughest foe
When Stratton hit Lincoln, oh what a hit
You could see after that the Chargers just quit
From" Looky, looky there goes Cookie"
To our corner store and our local bookie
After a loss how bad we'd all feel
We all felt much better after mom's homemade meal
Though the Rockpile is gone, it played a big part
And for that it will always be in our hearts

MY JOURNEY, MY GIFT

It's been a great Journey, that's for sure
It began as an infant, so tender and pure
I wonder why life can't stand stay
But God has a plan, so I listen and pray
Things happen for a reason, though we question why
The vision gets clearer as the years go by
Treat others like you want to be treated yourself
Never fear anything but fear itself
Trust in our Lord and follow his way
Try to say a prayer, at least one a day
I believe we are all sisters and brothers
Our gratification comes from helping others
Our lives could change just like the season
I do believe we were born for a reason
Do good deeds but do not boast
Your legacy is what you should cherish most
It's not how long you have to live
It's your quality of life and what you give
You may not cure cancer but there could come a day
You change someone's life in a different way
The Lord gives us a gift worth more than money
I make children laugh, they think I am funny
I try to bring sunshine amidst the rain
I help sick children forget their pain
I realize now right from the start
The gift I received was my heart

THANK YOU LORD

I open my eyes, it's a brand new day
I thank our dear Lord everything's okay
My heart starts pumping, I get out of bed
The blood starts rushing to my head
I'm feeling great, it's a beautiful morning
Each day is unique, it never gets boring
I use to complain but I don't anymore
I get dressed, eat breakfast, and then head out the door
Life is a gift that I appreciate so much
I know I've been blessed by our Lord's special touch
I see people suffer, and for them I pray
If I could I would help and show them the way
We take life for granted, that shouldn't be
We're just here for a while, until our soul is set free
I strive to do the best that I can
Reach out and give a helping hand
We all have potential, it's our choice to make
It's the chances in life we all must take
You should live every day like it was your last
Our lives fly by way too fast
So pray to sweet Jesus, he won't let you down
Put on your smile, don't wear your frown
The Lord will reward you if you are good
He'll love and protect you like only he could

JESUS WHERE ARE YOU

I see violence and hatred everywhere
We're in a bad war, do you even care
Are you on our streets late at night?
Our kids have guns, it's a horrible sight
Everywhere I look I see the face of the devil
Our elected officials aren't on the level
Babies are born with HIV
Crack babies are born, how can this be
The elderly are scared, they bolt their doors
On our once safe streets are gang fights and wars
And by the way, what's the deal with curing cancer
For years we've been trying to find an answer
Marriages are failing and it's the kids that suffer
Aren't you supposed to be their buffer?
I pray every night, I want to do good
I want to believe if only I could
Where are you dear Lord, we cannot wait
The way we are going, I fear our fate
As I prayed last night the Lord spoke to me
He said' "Look very closely, it's me that you see
I'm your police, your fire fighters, I'm here every day
If you need help, I'll show you the way
I'm your rabbi, your minister and your priest
On Thanksgiving Day I am your feast
I am your sunshine, I'm the birds in the sky
I'm the stranger you met that just said hi
You must keep your faith and spread my word
You can make a difference, you will be heard
So next time you have your morning tea
Say a little prayer, and it's me you will see

A SOLDIERS LETTER FROM HEAVEN

I'll never forget the day I told her
"Mom, I'm going to Iraq, I am a soldier"
I'm proud to serve when I got my call
My folks looked sadder than I ever saw
We cried, then hugged, as we said our goodbyes
And I saw the fear in my brother's eyes
I said," Jake don't worry, I'll be fine, you'll see"
With tears flowing down he saluted me
I boarded my plane with my big army sack
Never once thinking I might not come back
I was stationed in Bagdad, the ninth platoon
The time really flew, I'd be home real soon
The letters from my family could fill a large truck
They told me they loved me and wished me good luck
Three more days and I was going home
The last thing I packed was my razor and comb
I was on night watch my very last night
When I saw the enemy in my sight
The next thing I knew they surrounded me
Flashes of light was all I could see
I felt some pain as the gunfire ceased
At that moment I felt I was at peace
I felt I was floating, then I saw this bright light
I felt like I was on this amazing flight
I then saw my body lying down on the ground
I saw soldiers talking, but there wasn't no sound
I then saw our Lord and began to cry
It was my last night, how could I die
It felt so serene, I began to feel better
I asked if I could write a farewell letter
The Lord said yes so I began to write
"Dear mom and dad, I lost my life last night
I'm not coming home but please don't be sad
I love you so much, mom and dad
I did my best to make you both proud
It's now the Lord's love that I have found
I'm at peace in heaven, it's great up here

There's no more fighting, there's nothing to fear
Jake you can have my room and my bed
You must stay strong, and with that being said
Even though I'm not there, we won't be apart
As long as you keep me close in your heart

A VETERANS DAY TRIBUTE

As I get ready to go to Iraq for two years
My family's at the airport, there are plenty of tears
I will miss my family, and my friends
But we must preserve freedom and make sure terrorism ends
Once in Iraq I was nervous for sure
I patrolled the village, the people looked poor
There was gunfire and bombs that filled the air
The people here didn't seem to care
People were friendly but I took nothing for granted
You never knew where a bomb was planted
This sweet little girl invited me in her house
The family looked scared, they were as quiet as a mouse
It was Christmas time but it didn't seem real
These people were happy to just have a meal
I gave this sweet girl my good luck bear
I wanted to show them I really did care
She gave me some water and a piece of bread
They gave me a hug then went to bed
She taught me a lesson, it's better to give
We think about presents, they just want to live
When my duty was over I was a much smarter man
I told the protesters we're doing the best that we can
When we burn our flag it makes me sore
We're all Americans, we support the war
Our freedom comes with a big price
Peace in the world that would be nice
If we back our troops this is my belief
That our dear Lord will be Commander in Chief

THE FINISH LINE

I've been around for a very long time
I can almost see the finish line
My life's been fulfilling, I've learned a lot
I'm very thankful for what I got
I wish I knew then what I know now
I'd do things different, though I don't know how
My body is older, I have to slow down
I can't do as much this I found
The knowledge I gained over the years
Gives me respect among my peers
My competitive racing is a thing of the past
I still like to run, though not as fast
My children are grown and of them I am proud
They're smart yet humble, they are not loud
In this new world, I do not fit
The science and technology I just don't get
I sometimes miss my childhood days
Life was much simpler in many ways
I had a great mother and a terrific dad
Life couldn't have been better when I was a lad
The lessons I learned many years ago
Are still with me today as I grow old
My bones sometimes ache, at times they creak
But my mind is sharp for knowledge I seek
Not coming in first is quite okay
It's the experiences I encountered along the way
I enjoy each moment, they're precious and few
I embrace each day because they're exciting and new

EIGHTEEN WHEELER

I jump in my truck, my clothes in a sack
In three or four days I'll be heading back
The motor's purring like a pussycat
I put on my shades then put on my hat
It's two in the morning and it's very cold
But I'll be real toasty when I hit the road
I check my tires, log the miles in my book
I give my trailer one more look
I get an early start so I can stop at the diner
Sausage and pancakes, what could be finer
As I drive through Vegas I knew every dealer
Everyone knew my eighteen wheeler
When I get to Denver I might stop for a bite
I love Buena Vista, it's a beautiful sight
There's nothing more scenic, it's a memory I'll keep
As I drive my rig along Pikes Peak
I'm lucky to be single and make a good buck
I like lots of girls but I love my truck
I've been to Vermont and across the Great Plains
I drive when it snows, I drive when it rains
I've been way up north, I've drove through the south
I been to the Mississippi, I've been to her mouth
Wherever I go I take my old phone
I'm only a phone call away from home
Don't ever feel sorry for my life
I chose my truck over a wife
So I'll keep on rolling for a few more years
I may stop in your state and have a few beers
I know someday I'll settle down
But for now I'll keep trucking from town to town

ANGEL ON MY SHOULDER

Life isn't easy, it gets tougher each day
Our world is changing, but not in a good way
They say you gain wisdom as you get older
I'm convinced there's an angel upon my shoulder
Decisions I made weren't always that good
They say count your blessings and maybe I should
I hurt people's feelings, what was I thinking
I feel I'm in quicksand and slowly sinking
I feel I'm at the end of my rope
It's overwhelming, it's so hard to cope
When things work out I ask how could this be
I realize now, there's an angel with me
As I travel a path, I know there'll be bumps
I must move on and take my lumps
I know we learn from our mistakes
Sometimes we must make our own breaks
When things don't go right in whatever you do
It's great to have an angel by you
I truly believe I wouldn't be here today
If I didn't listen to my angel one day
At times I couldn't really explain
I'd slip and fall but there was no pain
I can't imagine not having my angel there
To give wisdom, guidance and loving care
You can't go through life on your own
With your angel you'll never feel alone
So next time your problems seem out of sight
Your angel will be there to make things right

THROUGH MY EYES

The beauty I see through my eyes
Would fill a heart of any size
There is beauty around, that's for sure
It's everywhere and it's very pure
Through my eyes I can see love
I sometimes see an innocent dove
Nature is something I love to see
From beautiful flowers to an old oak tree
The dark green grass and the light blue sky
I know it's God's work, I don't question why
I know I have eyes for a reason
Maybe to see the change of seasons
The colorful leaves, the pure white snow
The stars at night or the bright moon glow
I get up each morning and look outside
I might go to the country or take a long ride
I've walked down some long and winding roads
I've gone to a pond and seen some toads
I've gone to a farm on a Saturday morn
One time I saw a calf being born
Sometimes there's sadness in my eyes
I often have tears when we say our goodbyes
There's nothing I cherish more than my sight
I pray to the Lord I'll see the light
I close my eyes and travel afar
To a faraway galaxy or a star
Sometimes when I fall asleep at night
I can see heaven and it's a glorious sight

TWILIGHT YEARS

My mind says yes but my body says no
I once ran fast, I now run slow
I once could swim across the lake
Just thinking back makes me ache
Today I move at a slower pace
And the mirrors no friend to this old wrinkled face
I can't remember what I did last night
I need thicker glasses for my failing sight
My hearings going but that's okay
There's not much to hear anyway
I do have some knowledge I'd like to share
But younger kids don't seem to care
I use to play sports, now I play chess
I sit a lot more and move a lot less
The twilight years are definitely here
Growing old and lonely is my biggest fear
Putting life in prospective helps me each day
Growing old is a very small price to pay
I'm getting older but I can't complain
Along with sunshine there comes some rain
The next time I have a minor ache
I'll thank the Lord I did awake
With the grace of God I should be here for a while
Through the good and bad I'll continue to smile

A FRIEND

A friend is someone who is there in need
Needs no recognition, just does a good deed
You can call them anytime, day or night
They'll always be there to make things right
When you're down on your luck they have your back
No problems too big, they give you no flack
They'll sometimes tell you what you don't want to hear
They're very honest, that's perfectly clear
Years can pass without seeing your friend
Yet they'll stick by you to the very end
Friends are like diamonds, precious and rare
There are very few, they're not everywhere
It's not how high on the social ladder
They are your friend, it don't really matter
They won't gossip and they won't judge
If they disagree they won't hold a grudge
It would be great if you could help them too
There's times that they might be feeling blue
It takes a while to gain someone's trust
Having a good friend is a must
Remember the good times that we had
How you helped each other when times were bad
I get on my knees every day
And thank God you're my friend to this very day

SNOW BIRD

It's cold outside, my bones are creaking
As I walk to work, my shoes are squeaking
It's so bitter cold, where are the birds
I have to move south, this is absurd
When I start my car the engine sounds rough
Jogging each morning is getting real tough
And getting to work is quite a chore
The days seem long, winter's a bore
I should have a hobby, I need something to do
If that's not enough, I now have the flu
It's very depressing as I brave the cold
And it will get much worse as I grow old
It's time for a change, I need some good weather
Even if the sun turns my skin to leather
At least I'll be warm, I won't have frostbite
I could actually go out and have fun at night
No more blizzards and changing snow tires
No more shivering around bon fires
I'll just put on some shorts and go for a run
Jogging on the beach is lots of fun
No more slipping on patches of ice
Not shoveling snow would be nice
Don't get me wrong, I shouldn't complain
Before you have pleasure, you must experience pain
Living in Buffalo is getting old
I'd rather have sunshine than darkness and cold
The people are great in our fair city
The leaves in fall are very pretty
I'd come back for summer, I wouldn't leave for good
Even though there are times I feel I should
A snow bird is what I'll probably be
I'll just follow the path the Lord made for me
Wherever that takes me that's where I'll go
I just pray it's where the warm winds blow

GOODBYE WINTER

The trees are bare, the grass is brown
It's been a long cold winter in our small town
It's still pretty chilly, there's snowflakes falling
Spring's almost here, I can hear the ducks calling
It's time to come out of hibernation
Spring is a revival, it's a celebration
Things come to life, everything's brighter
The days are longer, it's getting lighter
It's time to get out, the sky is so blue
I'll go for a walk or go to the zoo
No frozen toes or frozen fingers
It's amazing how long our winter lingers
It's almost over, I'm counting the days
I'll go to the beach and catch some rays
Some people say winter's not long
But personally I believe they are wrong
I'm really over shoveling snow
There's nothing to do, nowhere to go
I guess I'm just a warm weather guy
Why I live here, I don't know why
I'd much rather live where its 90 degrees
Instead I live here where all I do is freeze
As I cross country ski with a large winter coat
I'd trade them in for shorts and a boat
I'd much rather have summer all year
Just thinking of Florida brings me a tear
Some day in Florida at Disney I'll be
Instead of laying around watching TV
Just give me the ocean and crystal white sand
Mix in some sand for my Coppertone tan
You'll never again hear me complain
But if I stay in this cold, I will go insane

MARATHON 25

MY ACHILLIES HEEL
Two weeks from the race and I'm feeling great
The stars are aligned, I believe in fate
My training is done, yet there's one thing to do
I have to go buy new running shoes
The ones I have are looking real old
I feel I betrayed them if truth be told
I cast them aside like an old shoe
I bought a new pair, they looked so cool
The very next day I broke them in
I forgot about my old shoes, they were stored in a bin
I'm feeling real good, I'm running with zeal
Until this sharp pain in my left heal
The very next day I took my shoes back
Humility is something I do not lack
I begged for forgiveness, I put my old shoes on
I had this good feeling, we stared to bond
I was standing at the starting line
My trusty old shoes felt really fine
I was into the race, about mile three
That's when my heel started hurting me
I fell in this pothole at mile eighteen
It hurt so much, it was a bad scene
But I managed to get to mile twenty
My spirits were good, but I ached plenty
I ran on one leg to mile twenty three
I knew my old shoes wouldn't betray me
My bones were aching, my feet felt like bricks
I finally made it to mile twenty six
So here is the moral of my story
Without dad and my shoes there would be no glory

HEAVENS CALL

I picked up my phone then put it down
My eyes filled with tears, there wasn't a sound
It was then I realized my mother was gone
She's up in heaven where she truly belongs
Every night I would call to hear moms voice
But now she's an angel and with our Lord she'll rejoice
When I had questions I'd call my mother
She understood me like no other
I think of our phone calls every day
She'd calm my fears, she knew the way
I wish she could call me from heaven above
I miss you mom, I send you my love
I'm happy you're finally rid of your cancer
If love was the cure, we'd have an answer
Mom you're my hero, you fought that disease
Now you can rest, you're finally at ease
The legacy you left is our family's love
I can feel you smiling from heaven above
You gave us your trust and a mother's protection
You pointed us in the right direction
You're still in our hearts though you have departed
And we will continue what you have started
I think of you mom when the telephone rings
I envision you with your angel wings
We no longer talk on the telephone
But with you in my heart I am not alone
I feel serenity because I know you're alright
And know that you'll be in my prayers every night

MY CHRISTMAS JOURNEY

It was Christmas Eve and all through our house
No one was moving, not even my spouse
But the scent of Christmas was in the air
It wasn't snowing and this was quite rare
All our stockings were hung, our tree looked great
My stomach felt queasy from the cookies I ate
I used my last tape and wrapping roll
The stress from Christmas was taking a toll
The turkey was thawing while the yams were soaking
Christmas was coming, there was no time for joking
When I get to the mall, there's no parking spots
When I spend all my money, I ask Is that all I got
The toy I wanted was gone days ago
Not going insane is now my main goal
Just when I think I can't take any more
I had to go to one more store
I'm very exhausted and my car is parked far
It was then I decide to stop at a bar
I feel I deserve a Christmas Eve drink
I bought everything but the kitchen sink
I stumbled to my car, my battery was dead
I then saw this man all dressed in red
He was merry and jolly, right out of a fable
He started my car with his jumper cables
Before I could thank him, in a blink of an eye
He got into this sled and flew through the sky
I told this wild story to my wife and my dog
I then went to bed and slept like a log
Well you might not believe this, I can't wait till next year
To see that fat man and his seven reindeer

DEAR MR. PRESIDENT

For better or worse you are the man
It's you who must lead us in our great land
We pray for you to make the right choices
AS commander in chief you are our voice
You have to be tough, make good decisions
Don't be afraid, you must follow your vision
We've been stuck in neutral way too long
Our days of prosperity are long gone
We do have a voice and we must be heard
Even if our problems seem absurd
Our country was built on courage and trust
Our American solders gave us their blood and guts
We must stay united no matter our race
We can't be divided by color of our face
It's good to look back but our future is now
We must work together, you must show us how
Your honeymoon is over, it's now time to work
The responsibilities you have you cannot shirk
We're losing our jobs and our self esteem
It can't get much worse or so it would seem
You have four short years to get this thing going
To jumpstart our lives and get our economy flowing
Most of all we want to live in peace
An end to all wars, the killing must cease
We must once again become a great nation
When the world's at peace there'll be a celebration
Let our Lord guide you, he's there in your heart
It's then our great nation won't be driven apart
You must work hard Mr. President
It's then that the message of "peace" can be sent

BEAUTY WITHIN

Beauty's skin deep and it would be a sin
Not to find the beauty that lies within
Remember in high school when looks were the thing
The prettiest girl would get your ring
Your teenage years when your face broke out
Your girlfriend would dump you, there was little doubt
You could be smart or a nice guy
If you weren't good looking it was often bye, bye
Peer pressure was tough and the girls could be cruel
But the guys could be superficial too
At times your looks could get you in trouble
You'd date a nice girl and she'd burst your bubble
As the years went by it got plainer to see
It's what's in your heart that mattered to me
There will come a time your good looks will fade
When you find your true love you'll have it made
Looks are deceiving but I wouldn't know
I'm pretty much average as far as looks go
But they say I have personality
I live my life in reality
Girls find my witty and charming too
I know my limitations, I am no fool
I love little children and respect the old
I have a good heart I am told
I'm happy just being an average guy
In an average life I try to get by
I have been blessed, I can't complain
There are people worse off, I feel their pain
My life is great and I don't take this for granted
I live every day where my roots have been planted

APOSTROPHE

Apostrophe this
Apostrophe that
No comma for me, that's not where it's at
Apostrophe's are cool, they make me look smart
Mar knew they were comas, but didn't have the heart
So, Mar told Donna to just let it go
Lar needed his commas to make his poems flow
We'll only confuse him, so we'll just let it be
I never found out and the rest is history

CAMP MEMORIES

When I look back in ninety-two
My life would change my priorities too
I went to CAMP GOOD DAYS on Keuka Lake
After a week with these kids my body would ache
These kids are so special that goes without saying
When I get home, I started praying
These beautiful children were stricken with cancer
I prayed to our lord to find an answer
My first year at camp was something to behold
I knew I was hooked if the truth be told
As we got our day's schedule there, I sat
When I noticed this man with this funny red hat
He didn't say much but he was well respected
When I saw him with children, I was really affected
He always had a child upon his back
Humor and charisma, he did not lack
I'll never forget the words he said
When the kids spilled cold water over my head
He said "you'll be here many many years"
As we hugged goodbye, I fought back the tears
He must have known something it's two thousand seven
I'm still going to camp though Craig's now in heaven
I lost some friends that I loved a lot
But I learned some lessons I never forgot
We're here for these children for only a week
We make a small difference but it's fun that we seek
One morning as we pushed this boat off the shore
Craig said "fall in the water the children will roar"
At that very moment a counselor I became
With these children I knew I'd never be the same
Fishing with Charlie and my little friend Drew
There was Sister Fran and Fritz was there too
There was Michael, Nick, and my good friend Matt
There was Graham from England in his cute British hat
From our opening prayers to our closing song
I'll always love camp it's where I belong

JUST A COUNSELOR

If I was a doctor and found cancers cure
I'd be a hero that's for sure
But I'm just a counselor I help tie kids laces
Give horsy rides and paint the kids' faces
I'm not a doctor I never went to college
But when it comes to these kids, I do have some knowledge
Doctors and nurses are these kids guiding light
But at camp we're the ones who tuck them in at night
Hospitals and medicine, they have their place
But it's at camp where you'll see a smile on their face
For a week there's no needles no pain or fuss
The tears only flow when they leave on the bus
As a counselor you need a special touch
These kids have taught me so very much
When I jog by the Craig Lawrence track each day
I turn my hat backwards and begin to pray
Craig, please help me be the best counselor I could be
And like you please never make this about me
Get me thru the week and with any strength I lack
Please give me the energy to put a child on my back

UNSUNG HERO'S

I've been with camp good days for 20 years
With the children at camp we share laughter and tears
As counselor's we play such a small part
When camp is over it tugs at the heart
Their parents look happy and thank us so much
But these parents are the ones with that special touch
We have their kids for one short week
There's no needles or doctors it's just fun we seek
We see them happy for five fast days
But their parents are there for hospital stays
They rarely show it but there's sorrow they share
Their love for their children is beyond compare
The problems they share we don't realize
But the bond with their kids you see in their eyes
I've met doctors and lawyers they are wealthy
But they'd trade it all if their child could be healthy
Each year at camp as we light a candle
I pray the lord don't give them more than they can handle
When I meet their parents, I see patience and love
And I see their faith in Jesus above
They're with their children twenty-four seven
And there's a special place for them in heaven

COUNTRY BOY

I'm a small-town boy with a big town smile
I'm no city slicker but they say I have style
Some people have called me a country bumpkin
But I have country manners, so I guess that means something
I married my first love, sweet Peggy Sue
We've been together since early high school
I still drive my four-speed black pickup truck
I have four wheel drive I never get stuck
Family comes first that goes without saying
And each Sunday at church the whole town is praying
We have a safe town we don't lock the doors
And we all do our shopping at ma and pa stores
Friday night football and sweet apple pie
Sitting on our porch under a star filled sky
Life isn't perfect but it's just right for me
There's no better place I'd rather be

WINTERS OVER

The snow has melted, winter is over
I'm a bit wiser, and one year older
Spring has arrived, bringing us flowers
No more long, cold, winter hours
I feel reborn, everything's growing
Instead of the snow drifting and blowing
The sun is so bright, the sky is so blue
Like the fresh green grass, we start anew
The long winters months, were dreary and cold
The journey is over, it was a long road
My energy level is now really high
I feel as free as the birds in the sky
My blood is flowing, like a fast flowing stream
Everyone's happy or so it does seem
I must not look back, like spring I must change
There's things in my life I must rearrange
Life springs eternal, I must follow my heart
I can take some advice, but I must do my part
The Lord gives the birds wings, but they must learn to fly
The Lord gave me talents, but it's me who must try
The long dark winter, is now a bright spring
Like music in my heart, I hear the birds sing
The next time you're blue, on a cold winter day
Let the Lord guide you and you will find your way

FLAGLER BEACH

It was the night before Christmas, on Flagler Beach
The moon was bright, the stars were in reach
The waves were big as they crushed the shore
We wore our shorts, it was seventy four
The sand was orange, the sky was clear
The sound of the waves, is all that we hear
Santa is seen flying over the ocean
I hope he brought us some sun tan lotion
Our families are not with us, it is pretty sad
Because time with our family, are the best times that we had
As I recall Christmas memories down my cheek ran a tear
Just then I see Santa and eight tiny reindeer
I believe there's a Santa, call me insane
But we're waiting for him to arrive at Renn Lane
There's no snow on our lawn, but we don't much care
It's Christmas in Flagler, there's peace in the air
When you visit our beach, you'll have no doubt
That the spirit of Christmas is what it's all about

HAIKU POEMS

Life gave you lemons
A dark cloud is over you
You will overcome

A monarch flew by
I knew it was my mother
She glides me through life

I danced through the streets
It was a glorious day
This is my true wealth

Was it dark out side
Were birds flying in the sky
I wish I could see

Birds flew up above
What is their destination
Is it peace they seek

Walking in the woods
The silence was deafening
Nature is calling

I looked in the mirror
Was that my true reflection
What is my future

Life is a picture
The true worth is up to us
Make it a Van Gough

You must have a goal
Did you ever have a dream
Wish upon that star

It was dark outside
Toads and crickets were singing
The concert was free

Trust is just a word
Your heart will tell you the truth
Look deep in my eyes

Spread your eagle wings
You fly through the sky with grace
We can learn from you

The old man was sad
Can I wipe your tear old man
Why must we get old

Enjoy every day
This is the best it will be
Tomorrow can wait

You made this our home
I can feel the love and warmth
Welcome Mary Beth

Each grape was unique
Good wine, good cheese and good friends
Every day is grape

The wise man once said
Open your eyes, close your mouth
He taught me so much

The candle burning
Our internal flame burns bright
My heart yearns for you

You say I am vain
I say it is confidence
I am not cocky

I never had sight
I see your face in my heart
You are so pretty

The blue bird flew by
Can I find serenity
Only time will tell

You are who you are
You are here for a reason
Do not waste your life

Pour a cup of love
Take a second slice of life
You get but one chance

Do not be afraid
Come out of your comfort zone
Take a baby step

Life can be complex
Your life can be a puzzle
Always trust your heart

TV, radio
How much bad news can we take
I just want to laugh

Our mom and our dad
They are like bread and butter
They need each other

Grass grows under us
Dew in the morning smells good
Our Lord at work

I saw my shadow
I will n ever be alone
You are my best friend

It was damp outside
The cold went right through my bones
Life can be chilly

I hope you believe
Faith does not need to be seen
Let the Lord guide you

Lead me down the path
I know that I can trust you
You are my Savior

Take me out to sea
Let me get lost in the stars
The moon is so bright

Raindrops are falling
The clouds are bursting above
I see the sunshine

The code of silence
I sing like a canary
I sleep with the fish

You are my family
Blood is thicker than water
I am here for you

I got up one night
Where is my Dutch apple pie
Boy it was yummy

Good night my sweetheart
May your dreams be a journey
Wake up my angel

Tiamo My Mar
I am potso for your love
Me monkey each day

I never could see
I heard the crickets chirping
The forest was dark

Buffalo may rock
Palm Coast is so super cool
Only one is my home

Snow fell on my face
My cheeks and nose are frozen
Winter has arrived

The grace of a swan
I was born with two left feet
I wish I could dance

The tears were flowing
I will only cry today
My last tear has dropped

You entered my soul
My body is full of you
Cancer you must leave

I ran my best race
Never did I look behind
My journey is done

My glass of red wine
Two candles by the bed side
We share our bodies

The hot steamy sun
Sweet dripping down my cheekbones
The ocean breeze feels great

A child is God's work
Raising our children is ours
How will they turn out

What color are you
It should not really matter
I am color blind

The snow was falling
Every snowflake was unique
Just like all of us

The sky opened up
A large bolt flashed through the sky
The clouds are crying

The door was open
Should I walk in or walk out
The sign said welcome

They hiked the football
Our warriors had one chance
What would be their fate

Communication
Our silence can be golden
I can read your face

The glow of your face
I wish I could read your mind
Tell me you love me

Pain is in your mind
Keep running that marathon
Your goal is in reach

It was early morn
The sun peaked through the window
My journey begins

The road kept winding
My whole body was aching
I must keep running

Why are we fighting
We are all one human race
Love should be our goal

In the midst of life
We encounter some crossroads
Which way will we go

The yellow brick road
Should be imaginary
If you let it be

The hot sultry sun
Shined directly on the sand
Each and every grain

The ball floated down
As I waited in left field
What would be my fate

The sky was so blue
The roller coaster creaked up
The journey began

The leaves drifted down
As the ground swallowed them up
All covered with dew

Footprints in the sand
Could it be a long-lost friend
Only time will tell

I live in darkness
Yet I can see the birds fly
How lucky am I

The beast showed his head
I will slay him with my sword
You must die cancer

When life seems bleak
Go to the river and fish
The world is not bad

As I walk the path
There are many obstacles
But I must not fail

If life was an orange
I would squeeze out all the juice
Then drink it all up

Wisdom without love
Is like birds without their wings
A necessity

The man in the moon
Does anyone know his name
Does anyone care

Books, books everywhere
The vast array of knowledge
Libraries are cool

I looked in his eyes
My horse was ready to run
He never looked back

Life is on a thread
Live like it is your last day
Conquer all your fears

The spider looked huge
Would he spin an evil web
Only he would know

Be very quiet
Walk softly through the forest
Hear the branches crack

I like to run uphill
Only the strong shall survive
I will run the race

The fish swam up stream
The current was very strong
The journey was rough

Leaves fell to the ground
The colors were majestic
Which way will they fall

The waves were crashing
The high tide swallowed the shore
Treasure on the beach

The sword is mighty
The pen is much mightier
My poems will slay

No time for bad news
Our journey has but two paths
I take the high road

Tears on my pillow
Tears of joy to be alive
What a gorgeous day

I looked through the cage
Would someone please adopt me
I am a good dog

We saw right through you
Cancer is predictable
We will find a cure

Your voice was so soft
Your skin as soft as velvet
You are quite a girl

We fished off the pier
The fish were biting today
In it to win it

I ran down the beach
My sweaty achy calves cramped
Only ten more miles

The search for my love
It may take me a lifetime
Where is my angel

The blades of grass grew
The rain came down in buckets
Spring is finally here

I am in darkness
Will I ever see again
Lord show me the light

People walking fast
The whole world is in a rush
Just take a deep breath

My dog melts my heart
Love is unconditional
He is my best friend

I hear the whispers
I hear the bluebirds chirping
Life can be grand

Paint me a picture
Then let me walk into it
I want to get lost

Death is a blackhole
Where do we go when we die
We will all find out

The hot sultry sun
We walked barefoot in the sand
Your blue eyes sparkled

Cry me a river
Your tears can be tears of joy
Emotions run wild

FOREWORD

FIRST AND FOREMOST, I'D LIKE TO THANK A HIGHER
POWER FOR ALLOWING ME TO WRITE MY POEMS.
I TRULY AM BLESSED TO HAVE A SUPPORT
GROUP SECOND TO NONE.
WITHOUT ALL OF YOU, THIS BOOK WOULD NOT HAVE
BEEN POSSIBLE. MY FAMILY, MY MOM AND DAD, AND
FRIENDS WHO PUSHED ME TO PUBLISH MY BOOK.
MARY BETH, WHERE WOULD I BE WITHOUT YOUR CONFIDENCE
IN ME.? YOUR COMITMENT TO THIS BOOK MAKES THIS
BOOK YOURS AS MUCH AS MINE.I LOVE YOU VERY MUCH.
PEOPLE IN MY LIFE WHO INSPIRED ME I THANK YOU, MY SONS
CHRISTOPHER, JONATHAN (MARIA), MY GRANDCHILDREN.
ANGELINA, ALDO, PARKER AND TANNER WHO ARE ALSO
MY GRANDCHILDREN, SHIRLEY AND TONY. MY PASSION
CAME EASY, THE SUBJECTS WERE ALL I NEEDED, THE
ONLY PROBLEM I HAD WAS TYPING ALL THESE POEMS.
I WROTE ABOUT LIFE, FICTION, AND NONFICTION. I WROTE
WHAT WAS IN MY HEART. YOU ALL KNOW ME, I DON'T TAKE
MY SELF TOO SERIOUSLY, I WRITE INSPIRATIONAL, SAD,
HAPPY, FUNNY, WHATEVER SUITED MY MOOD THAT DAY
IF YOU CAN TAKE JUST ONE OF MY POEMS AND RELATE
TO IT, THAT WOULD MAKE MY BOOK A SUCCESS.
IT TOOK MANY YEARS TO WRITE THESE POEMS, IT
TOOK ABOUT THREE MONTHS TO PUT TOGETHER.
MY HOPE IS YOU LAUGH, CRY, MAYBE GET INSPIRED AND
POSSIBY LEARN A LITTLE MORE ABOUT YOURSELF.
AS MY PEN MOVES FASTER THAN MY THOUGHTS,
IT SOMETIMES WAS HARD TO READ WHAT I JUST
WROTE. IT WAS A ROLLER COASTER RIDE TO BE SURE,
ONE I WOULDN'T CHANGE FOR THE WORLD.
I'LL BE HAPPY TO SELL JUST ONE BOOK OR ONE HUNDRED
BOOKS BECAUSE I STAYED TRUE TO MYSELF
AND DID NOT COMPROMISE MY BELIEFS. I JUST HOPE
I CAN TAKE YOU ON AN ADVENTURE AND GET YOU
LOST IN MY BOOK FOR A COUPLE OF HOURS.

AND YES LINDA, (FROM PAYROLL A T THE ERIE
COUNTY LIBRARY) I FINALLY FINISHED. THANK
YOU FOR BEING ONE OF MY BIGGEST FANS
TO DAWN AND DARLENE, GRAPHIC ARTS, ALSO THE ERIE
COUNTY LIBRARY THANK YOU FOR ALL YOUR HELP. I HAD LOTS
OF FUN WRITING MY HAIKU POEMS, HOPE YOU ENJOY THEM
A SPECIAL THANKS TO CAMP GOOD DAYS AND SPECIAL TIMES,
FOR KEEPING ME FOCUSED, INSPIRED AND HUMBLE.
SO HAVING SAID ALL THIS, SIT BACK, RELAX, LET
THE "JINGLE MAN" TAKE YOU ON AN ADVENTURE
OF A LIFE TIME. I HOPE YOU ENJOY READING THESE
POEMS AS MUCH AS I ENJOYED WRITING THEM.

THE JINGLE MAN
LARRY

Printed in the United States
By Bookmasters